ALL SERIOUS DARING STARTS

BEGIN

HERE

FROM WITHIN.

EUDORA WELTY

Strictly Ballroom is the only movie where the rumba meets gold lamé intrigue meets the Australian suburbs. Our hero is Fran, and her *cri de coeur* is "a life lived in fear is a life half lived." It's brilliant.

DON'T REGRET A LIFE HALF LIVED

WHEN MY LAPTOP STARTS UP, IT DISPLAYS A DATE: SEPTEMBER 15, 2043. IT'S A DESTINATION: MY DEATH.

Kevin Kelly created the Death Date, the end point of a "countdown clock" that tells you your theoretical moment of demise, based on actuarial tables.

Kelly believes we can do one "big project" every five years. So, first publishing this book in 2022, and assuming that my Death Date is about right, I've got time left for *counts on fingers* about four big projects.

Do something that matters

You might be noticing the passage of time too. Maybe you're just starting off, or mid-career, or wrapping things up... and you feel the stirrings of new ambition. Maybe you're outraged by an injustice in society, or frustrated about the ways things are done in your organization, or restless about playing it safe. Maybe you're noticing that your life is full enough... but not as rich or as meaningful as you'd hoped.

Whatever your itch, I'm really glad you're here. The How to Begin process in this book will help you get going on a project of your own, something that matters.

MBS

MICHAEL BUNGAY STANIER

Mostly known as MBS... but obviously not the Saudi MBS, who is another kettle of fish altogether.

WE UNLOCK OUR

GREATNESS

BY WORKING ON

THE HARD THINGS.

SHALL WE START?

HOW TO

Michael Bungay Stanier

BEGIN

START DOING

SOMETHING

THAT MATTERS

● ● **PAGE TWO**

Cataloguing in publication information is
available from Library and Archives Canada.
ISBN 978-1-77458-058-5 (paperback)
ISBN 978-1-77458-059-2 (ebook)
ISBN 978-1-77458-196-4 (audiobook)

Page Two
pagetwo.com

Edited by Amanda Lewis
Copyedited by John Sweet
Proofread by Alison Strobel

Designed by Peter Cocking
Illustrations by Brian Tong

Printed and bound in Canada
Distributed in Canada by Raincoast Books
Distributed in the US and internationally by Macmillan

22 23 24 25 26   5 4 3 2 1

HowToBegin.com

Visit MBS.works for more information
about Michael Bungay Stanier's work.

TELL ME, WHAT IS IT YOU PLAN TO DO

WITH YOUR ONE WILD AND PRECIOUS LIFE?

MARY OLIVER, "THE SUMMER DAY"

HOW TO FIND YOUR WAY AROUND THIS BOOK

Someone once said I was the bastard child of Pixar's Mr. Incredible and the Muppets' Fozzie Bear. Honestly, there's been no higher compliment.

But it now seems unlikely that Pixar will create a character based on my life, so I've had to seize the moment and make one for myself. This little guy is me, MBS. He'll be popping up throughout the book to provide commentary on the process, stories, and guidance too.

INTRODUCTION

Be ambitious (twice)

When I first met Marcella, we'd both just arrived at Oxford University to study. She'd gone from being a high school dropout to winning a scholarship to do a PhD there. (I know, pretty cool.) Tacked to the door in her dorm was a scrap of paper, and on it was printed "Life is not a dress rehearsal." Reader, I married her.

I love the lesson on that note. We all get one crack at this life, so make the most of it. Do something that matters. That means being doubly ambitious—for your life, and for the world.

Ambitious for your life means unlocking your greatness and becoming the best version of yourself. Science repeatedly tells us that happiness rarely comes from money or fame or status, even if you're lucky enough to have any of those; it comes from a life well lived. A life where you don't let fear or past scars or made-up BS get in the way of growing, refining and using your talents, exploring your edges, and having adventures. To fulfill this first ambition is no small thing, and it might be enough for some. But I want to offer an additional ambition that I hope you'll also hold.

Ambitious for the world might mean making headlines: starting an organization; inventing a technology; protesting against tyranny; populating Mars. But also consider it at a more intimate scale: building a better relationship; following through on a challenging deliverable; leading a thriving team; returning to study; making and sharing a creative project; chairing a community meeting. (For more inspiration, see the extended list on the inside cover.)

Ambition for the world means looking past your own happiness, and the test is "Will you give more to the world than you take?" No matter who you are, no matter how much privilege you do or do not have, you can find a way to give more to the world than you take.

These two ambitions amplify each other. By taking on the hard thing—I frame it in this book as your Worthy Goal—you step out to the edges of your skills and experience. You struggle and stumble, and you also figure it out, learn, and grow. You build capacity, wisdom, and confidence. You reveal and strengthen your Best Self as you do the work.

As you unlock your greatness by working on the hard things, you'll make a difference and you'll make the world a little better.

Now... be honest

There's a chance you're thinking: "I'm not sure if this book is for me. It sounds like it's for those who are... clearer on their goals, more privileged, less overwhelmed, more accomplished, further along, more activist, more established, less established, more or less selfish, older, younger, smarter, faster, braver" (and so on... you can insert your own reasons for why you're not quite ready). ←

One of my favourite monarchs is Æthelred the Unready, King of the English from 978 to 1013. I can relate. (To the unready bit. Less so to the "ruler" bit.)

You're right to feel a little unsure. A Worthy Goal is Thrilling, Important, and Daunting. Few people feel fully ready for that from a standing start. This book and the How to Begin process is for all those who feel both ambition and resistance.

This process will work for you...

No matter where you're located within society

You might be older or younger, established or just beginning, part of the mainstream or an activist, holding some of the cards of privilege or part of a group that's faced systemic barriers. The process here will meet you and greet you where you are.

No matter the focus and scale of your ambition

You might have big, bold, change-the-world dreams. Fantastic. You might be focused on something local. Perfect. You might be starting or scaling up a creative project. Excellent. This process holds space for the grand or intimate, global or local, entrepreneurial or organizational, disruptive or creative. There's room for all of that.

No matter where you are on the journey

You might already be in the middle of a Worthy Goal, and want some help refocusing and reigniting your commitment. You might be itching to start on something that you know is good, but you lack permission. You might still be searching for the right thing to start. All good, and all welcome here.

Here's what unites everyone who picks up this book: You sense the stirrings of your own ambition. You know that you have more to contribute. You want to shake things up and make a difference. You want to learn and grow. You want to use your power for good.

And you're ready to begin.

How to Begin

Let me give you a glimpse of what's ahead of you. The How to Begin process has three broad sections, each with three steps.

First, *Set a Worthy Goal*. I'll help you find and refine a goal that is Thrilling, Important, and Daunting. A Worthy Goal entwines ambition for yourself *and* for the world.

DON'T SHRINK FROM NEW EXPERIENCES AND CUSTOM. TAKE THE COLD BATH BRAVELY.

W.E.B. DU BOIS, LETTER TO HIS DAUGHTER

Second, *Commit*. You want to be clear and confident that this is a journey worth taking. Naming what's to be won and what's to be left behind will help steel your resolve.

Third, *Cross the Threshold* towards that Worthy Goal. Taking the first step leads to the next, then the next, and you make progress. You do need to get going. Being too scared to act on a Worthy Goal isn't just a loss to you, it's a loss to us all.

In the coming pages I'm going to break down this process bit by bit. You'll know exactly how it works, and be able to use it and reuse it. The process will be a practical tool that can help you now and in the future.

Yes, it's a process

Frankly, I love/hate processes. Maybe you do too.

A bad process is entirely frustrating. If it's too vague and high level, it's like stumbling around a stranger's living room in the dark: you're never quite sure where you're going, and you keep bumping into things that bruise your shins. If it's too tight and restrictive, you spend the whole time grudgingly picking the least bad options and looking to bail.

But a *good* process is a thing of beauty: it's loose enough that you can make it feel your own, and tight enough to save you from distractions; it gives you some of what you want, and reveals what you didn't know you needed; and it has an elegance and simplicity that makes it approachable, and engages enough with both theory and practical reality so it's not simplistic or fragile.

A good process is scalable. That means it's understandable, can be taught and learned, and can spread. You can take it, adapt it, and make it your own. You can use it by itself or work it through with others.

I've tested the process you're about to get into with thousands of people, and it works. But a process isn't a process *unless* you're working it. You must bring yourself and your ambitions to it.

How do you roll?

You've got options for how you work the process, all with pros and cons.

Who you do the process with

By yourself: Personal, private, and fast. You can move quickly and also "confess the sins" that you might not share with others. But it's also hard to access what you don't know you don't know, and it's all too easy to be slippery and let yourself off the hook.

With a partner: The shared sense of travel and vulnerability can be powerful and rewarding. But this method is typically slower than working solo, and less expert than working with a facilitator.

With a facilitator or coach: It can be a delight to have someone else hold the space for you, so you can lean in and fully give yourself to the process. But you have to find an adept guide you trust.

The speed at which you do the process

Fast: Going quickly can help you finish, without being bogged down or overthinking. Some of my most powerful insights have resulted when I've been moved faster-than-feels-comfortable through a process. But it's hard to go deep on any one place.

Slow: Going slowly allows deep dives and self-reflection. But it can mean you get stuck or have time to dodge the harder questions.

There's a worksheet if you want it

If you find this sort of structure helpful, there's a worksheet you can use. You can make a copy of the short-form one in the book (page 191) or download a PDF and/or access an online copy of this form or an

 expanded version at HowToBegin.com. Use the QR code to check out the online versions. (After 10 years, QR codes have finally started to work!)

HOW DO YOU ROLL?

If it's helpful, guess your preferred process now.

How long will this take? Probably about two to five minutes.

Who will you travel with?

_____

_____

_____

_____

What's your preferred speed of travel?

_____

_____

_____

_____

EXERCISE

LIFE IS SHORT.

SET A

START DOING SOMETHING

WORTHY

THAT MATTERS.

GOAL

SOMETHING THRILLING,

IMPORTANT, AND DAUNTING.

It's hard to be ambitious

I'm in my fifties, and one of the small but insulting ways my body's aged is that my eyesight's warped. I now spend too much time figuring out focal lengths, calculating... Should I be wearing regular glasses? Try to find my reading glasses? Dig out my contact lenses? Or maybe keep doing the squinty-hunch thing without any glasses at all?

Targeting our ambition can be like that: about to come into focus, before getting fuzzy again. It's hard to pin down because it is so often a slippery combination of exclusive, illusive, and elusive. ←————— Who doesn't love a good homonym? You're welcome.

Exclusive, because it can seem that ambition is only for those people who've been dealt the cards of privilege. I'm one of them, as it happens, and I'd say that, even with the hand I'm holding, it can still be a struggle at times. It's harder still if you don't have those cards, and that means...

- It's harder if you're not male.
- It's harder if you're not white (at least in North America and Europe).

- It's harder if you're not cis and heterosexual.
- It's harder if you don't have a "tribe."
- It's harder if you've had a disrupted childhood.
- It's harder if... well, the list is long.

Illusive, because we're living at a time when the bling of self-centred accomplishment seems bigger and shinier than ever. Social media is filled with highlight reels. Whatever your dreams, you can find someone to envy: more stuff, more reach, more power. If this type of success is all you pursue, beware: when you reach the top of your mountain, you will discover it's not the peak you hoped it would be.

David Brooks →
talks about
this in his book
*The Second
Mountain*.

Elusive, because even if you can own your ambition and ensure it serves both you and the world, it can still be hard to articulate. You need to hold on to what you'd like to achieve, who you'd like to be, and how you might be a force for change.

Where are you now?

Take a moment to gauge what might get in the way of you claiming your ambition. There's no wrong answer here; it's purely to help you see where you stand.

☐ **Not yours** You might have the beginnings of something, but the goal feels as if it's been inherited, or borrowed from someone else, or accidentally adopted. It's like a spontaneous tattoo you got at 3 a.m. after a fun

DON'T UNDERTAKE A PROJECT UNLESS IT IS MANIFESTLY IMPORTANT AND NEARLY IMPOSSIBLE.

EDWIN LAND

night out with your friends: it's slightly dodgy, you can't quite remember the details of how you ended up saying yes to this, you don't really want it, but you feel stuck with it now, so... oh well.

☐ **Not allowed** You might feel that you're not allowed to have a Worthy Goal. There's a "You have to be *this tall* to go on this ride" sign, and you keep coming up a few inches too short. Perhaps you're what Minda Harts calls "the first and the only," so there's no one who's gone before you to show you how; or you've been told too often that having those ambitions is not for someone like you; or not just yet, come back later; or you're close but not quite ready or deserving... and you have come to believe it yourself.

☐ **Not moving** You might feel you've found the Worthy Goal, made a start, and somehow wandered off the path. Now you find yourself slogging ankle deep through a swamp, battling insects and a really unpleasant smell, feeling tired and discouraged, and wondering how exactly you ended up here.

☐ **Not yet emerged** You might have a sense of your ambition, but you haven't found an outlet for it yet. That ambition might burn bright and hard, or it might be shy and quiet... but you know it's there, and when it finds its home, cool things are going to happen.

Wherever you are, that's perfect. Because no matter where you are, now can be a time to find and refine your Worthy Goal.

You're worth it

Google "Viola Davis + L'Oréal" for a particularly fabulous version of this classic advertising line.

To find your Worthy Goal, you need to interrogate the possibilities. It must be worthy of *you*: your time, your focus, your resources and resourcefulness. Your Worthy Goal must be worth your life. Your life!

In this first part of the How to Begin process, you work through *three drafts of your Worthy Goal*. It is rigorous because I want you to feel confident that the Worthy Goal really matters to you. Only then can you maintain your drive, stay the course, overcome the barriers and difficulties, and make progress that matters on this adventure.

SET A WORTHY GOAL

You are here

1 FIND YOUR FOCUS
WRITE A CRAPPY FIRST DRAFT

2 TEST YOUR AMBITION
WRITE AN ACTIVE SECOND DRAFT

3 CLAIM YOUR GOAL
WRITE A STRONG FINAL DRAFT

COMMIT

4 SEE WHERE YOU STAND
FALSE STARTS & MOSQUITOES

5 WEIGH UP THE STATUS QUO
COMFORTS & COSTS

6 WEIGH UP THE JOURNEY
QUALITIES & RISKS

CROSS THE THRESHOLD

7 TAKE SMALL STEPS
HISTORIES, EXPERIMENTS & PRACTICES

8 REMEMBER YOUR BEST SELF
THIS/NOT THAT

9 DON'T TRAVEL ALONE
BUILD THE BAND

HOW TO BEGIN

IN THIS CHAPTER

THE THREE ELEMENTS

OF A WORTHY GOAL

1 FIND YOUR FOCUS

Setting the standard

"Set a *Worthy* Goal." Sheesh. Worthy is a *big* word. It can feel a little... earnest. Perhaps a little high and mighty. You might be thinking, "Who am I to be measuring things on a level of *worthiness*?" But "worthy" is less about an abstract moral rating and more about whether it's worthy enough for *you* to be committing to it.

Worthy becomes more accessible as a standard when you understand its three different elements: Thrilling, Important, and Daunting. They're the primary colours that allow you to paint the picture of your ambition. If you have all three of these in a goal or a project, you've got something intriguing on your hands.

Thrilling

The idea of taking this on gets you going. You're *excited* about this, not just in theory but in real life. *Thrilling* means something to you. It speaks to your values and lights up your receptors. It makes you rub your hands together and think: "YES! This!" You'd be proud to do this. It's cool, fun, bold. It's an adventure you want to have.

Thrilling is a countermeasure against a sense of obligation. The tendrils of expectations—others' and our own—can keep us rooted to the spot. "I *should* be doing/wanting/achieving/claiming this..." is a heavy stone that many of us carry.

Important

In Jacqueline Novogratz's wonderful book *Manifesto for a Moral Revolution*, she lays down the challenge to "give more to the world than you take." *Important* connects to that. It's a project or a goal that's for a bigger win than just self-satisfaction or self-gratification. The stakes are higher than your life.

Part of the power of Novogratz's phrase comes from its scalability. You're giving more to the world than you're taking if you're working on a key relationship at home, cracking that challenging work project, starting a book or podcast, going back to school, starting a neighbourhood group, beginning as a solopreneur, protesting against injustices, inventing technologies, or a thousand other Worthy Goals.

Important is a countermeasure against selfishness. I'm all for investing in yourself, personal exploration, and growth, but for the most part, "self-help" is not sufficient to create a better world.

Daunting

With *Daunting*, when you think about taking this on, there's a flutter in your heart (or ⟵ your stomach, or your shoulders, depending on where you show tension). It docsn't feel utterly impossible, nor is it immediately obvious how you're going to get going on this or finish it. If the thought of taking on this goal makes you just a little bit sweaty, then you're nudging up to *Daunting* in an interesting way.

I jiggle my right leg when I'm feeling under pressure. I can trace it back to the experience of learning piano with Mrs. "Knuckle-Rapper" Birmingham.

Daunting is a countermeasure against the comfort zone. Endless influences encourage you to grind it out, play it safe, and keep it small. *Daunting* helps banish those by inviting you back to the learning edge.

Two out of three?

What if your Worthy Goal ticks only two of the three qualities? Isn't that close enough? Well, it might be. But like a three-legged stool with one leg shorter than the others, it's probably usable but slightly precarious.

There's a helpful tension between Thrilling and Important. They're two hands stretching a rubber band. In that state, there's dynamic potential. But let one of them go, and the potential is lost.

Here's how the interactions play out:

I first heard this metaphor from management writer and artist Robert Fritz.

Important and Daunting but not Thrilling

This Worthy Goal will feel a little too *obligated*. It's worthy work that stretches you and contributes to a better world, but it doesn't nourish you and isn't interesting enough to sustain you. There's the danger of burnout here.

Thrilling and Daunting but not Important

This Worthy Goal will feel a little too *self-centred*. It's exciting work that will stretch and grow you, but the "why" of the work is for you rather than also contributing to others. Don't write off small, more intimate, personal projects... but do find a way to connect them to the wider world. There's a risk of "Why bother?" here.

Thrilling and Important but not Daunting

This Worthy Goal will feel a little too *comfortable*. It's solid work and might have once stretched you, but now you're in cruise control. You might start to stagnate if you stay here too long.

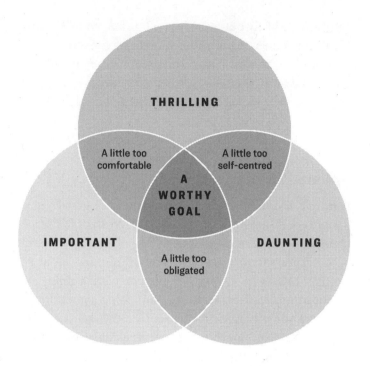

DON'T SETTLE FOR TWO OUT OF THREE

Three dimensions

With Thrilling, Important, and Daunting established
as the base, you're ready to look for your Worthy Goal.
Now, you may already have your Worthy Goal sketched
out. You've just been waiting for a nudge and permission
to get going. That's great... and even though you might
be tempted, don't skip this section. The very worst
thing that happens is you confirm you've totally nailed it.

And a more likely outcome is you'll refine your Worthy Goal and make it even more compelling for you.

But if you're a little more uncertain, where do you start? Here are three different but intersecting dimensions—sphere, scale, and class—where you might shine a light and explore.

Sphere: Work & Not Work

A simple way to begin is to split the world into two spheres of possibility: Work and Not Work. If it's something to do with an organization (big or small), or being an entrepreneur, or part of a team, or thinking about a product or service, it might fit in Work. If it's about a relationship, or creating and/or launching something, or studying something new, or a social cause, or a contribution to a neighbourhood, or serving your tribe in some way, it might be Not Work.

Don't get overly hung up on the language. I know there are other ways to cut this cake, and that there's not always a clear distinction between the two. I also know that it doesn't *totally* matter what you put in one bucket and what you put in another. For instance, if you're a student, and you want to put your performance at school into Work, or into Not Work, the choice is yours. It's just a lens that can help you see options and opportunities.

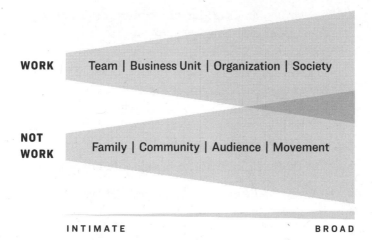

WORK	Team | Business Unit | Organization | Society
NOT WORK	Family | Community | Audience | Movement

INTIMATE   BROAD

Scale: Intimate to Broad

Within the Work and Not Work spheres, you can engage in different levels of scale. You might choose to narrow your attention, focus on something intimate, and work close and tight. Or you might sweep more broadly and dream more expansively. Neither one is better or worse than the other. Thrilling, Important, and Daunting remain the measures that matter.

Scale in the Work sphere

For Work, one way of mapping the scale from intimate to broad is:

- The *team*'s leadership, projects, commitments, and interactions within the team and between other teams.

- The *business unit*'s leadership, commitments, and interactions with other business units.

- The *organization*'s strategy and culture.

- How the organization meets, influences, and serves *society*.

Scale in the Not Work sphere

For Not Work, an intimate-to-broad scale might be this:

- How the *family* nurtures and loves and evolves.

- What's required for a *community* to be inclusive and resilient and resourced.

- The creative work that can move an *audience*.

- A *movement* that transcends geography and/or community and/or audience.

Class: Projects, People & Patterns

Infused throughout Work and Not Work is another framework. You can choose, within whatever context is calling you, to focus on Projects, People, or Patterns. (The three are of course completely interconnected. You're just choosing to put one particular class into the foreground.)

Projects. The most common type of Worthy Goal. A project is something that needs to be done, and it typically has a start and a finish, a sense of done or not done, a number of steps to move you from here to there, and success or failure. You'll be getting dirt under your fingernails, even if it's just digital dirt from working the keyboard. Project-class Worthy Goals have a primary focus on Doing.

People. We are always "in relationship." It's impossible to imagine someone who exists outside a web of connections. We're shaped by who we love and by whom we're loved, who we lead and who we follow, who we transact with and with whom we play. Sometimes the Worthy Goal is to bring your focus to one or more of those relationships— to be a better and different brother, manager, friend, partner, daughter, client, founder, caregiver, vendor. It's you and that other person. People-class Worthy Goals have a primary focus on Interacting.

David Allen's book *Getting Things Done* first introduced me to the power of projects. Bottom line: get the thoughts out of your head and into a system you can trust— and, where you can, make them a project.

Patterns. This is when you hold up the mirror and interrogate how you're showing up in the world. Are your current patterns of behaviour still serving you well? Do you need to leave behind an old way of being and doing that doesn't fit your ambition? It doesn't always feel as though you can connect Patterns to Important, but breaking through to be the next-best version of yourself really does give more to the world than it takes. Pattern-class Worthy Goals have a primary focus on Being.

BRAINSTORM SOME POSSIBILITIES

If it's helpful, you can sketch some initial possibilities of a Worthy Goal in this chart. I'd encourage you to put down two, three, or more possibilities (even if you're pretty sure what your Worthy Goal will be). Seeing the options will help you weigh up choices.

How long will this take? Probably about 10+ minutes.

EXERCISE

SPHERE	WORK	NOT WORK	
SCALE	INTIMATE · · · · · ● ● ●		BROAD
CLASS	PROJECT	PEOPLE	PATTERN

_____

_____

_____

SPHERE	WORK	NOT WORK	
SCALE	INTIMATE · · · · · ● ● ●		BROAD
CLASS	PROJECT	PEOPLE	PATTERN

_____

_____

_____

As ongoing examples for you, I've added two of my own Worthy Goals, which I'll be working through the How to Begin process. I'll explain more in a few pages.

SPHERE	WORK	(NOT WORK)	
SCALE	INTIMATE · · · · · · ·(●)		BROAD
CLASS	(PROJECT)	PEOPLE	PATTERN

MBS's Worthy Goal 1
Create a new, top-notch podcast

As you can see, I've circled Not Work for the sphere, a dot close to Broad for the scale, and Project for the class.

SPHERE	(WORK)	NOT WORK	
SCALE	INTIMATE ·(●)· · · · · ●		BROAD
CLASS	PROJECT	(PEOPLE)	(PATTERN)

MBS's Worthy Goal 2
Stop being CEO of Box of Crayons

This Worthy Goal is in the Work sphere, the scale is fairly Intimate, and, for the class, I've circled both People and Pattern.

This is true of every first draft

I'm not the first to say it, but I can attest to its truth: the first draft is *always* crappy. The first time I write anything, it's thoroughly mediocre. It's tepid and confused. It's overstuffed and underbaked. It's too specific and too vague, all at once. "Funny" but not in a way that's at all amusing. It's overloaded with metaphors, like a sausage about to split its casing, or a circus with a surfeit of clowns, or a hamster playing drums. It goes on and on trying to make the point, never knowing when to stop, hoping that one more phrase will make it better. This paragraph is a case in point.

I first heard "shitty first draft" from the brilliant Anne Lamott. Brené Brown suggests "stormy" as a gentler adjective.

The same is true when you begin to claim a Worthy Goal. It's almost impossible to nail it first time around. There are any number of reasons. We fumble after the right language. We diminish our own ambition because it's easier to write down something small. Or the opposite happens, and we overwhelm our ambition by writing something too abstract or overblown: "Find happiness."

But we have to start somewhere, and when we start with full permission to write down a crappy first draft, it's something. Actually, it's more than something—it's a significant and critical first step.

You might be hesitating. Yes, it's awkward. No, it won't be perfect. But take your best guess. It will set you up for the next step, where we'll take what you've written and make it stronger and better.

WRITE A CRAPPY FIRST DRAFT
OF YOUR WORTHY GOAL

Don't overthink it. You'll have a chance to redraft it shortly.
How long will this take? Probably up to five minutes.

EXERCISE

_____

_____

_____

_____

I'm along for the ride

Look, I don't want you to do anything I wouldn't do
myself. I'm going to work through my own process with
two real Worthy Goals for me. Why two? Because I want
you to see two different types of Worthy Goals, different
in focus and scale and type. My examples always follow
the invitation to do your own, so you don't get unduly
influenced, though you're welcome to look ahead and
steal/adapt/borrow anything you see in my work for
your own. There are also two other case studies in the
Pilot Light (the book's appendix), completed by real
people from the MBS.works community who've been
kind enough to share their process with you.

Turn the page for my first drafts.

SPHERE	WORK	(NOT WORK)	
SCALE	INTIMATE · · · · · · ●(●)	BROAD	
CLASS	(PROJECT)	PEOPLE	PATTERN

Here's my crappy first draft of a Worthy Goal that's real and alive for me as I write this (early 2021):

Create a new, top-notch podcast

When I showed a first draft of this book to my inner circle, I got a bunch of comments about how this didn't feel much like a Worthy Goal for me. After all, I've launched podcasts before. I was accused, nicely-ish, of wimping out and playing it safe.

Here's why it's a Worthy Goal. First, it's not a Work project. I want this to be something that's fulfilling for me creatively, not just a marketing side project. Second, I want this podcast to be successful and different. I don't want to just "phone it in" by doing an interview with some inter-esting folk. I want this to be a serious upgrade. I want to become a masterful podcaster.

Most importantly? You're the final judge of what is and isn't a Worthy Goal for you. Feedback is not the truth. It's potentially helpful, but not necessarily so.

EXAMPLE

SPHERE	(WORK)	NOT WORK					
SCALE	INTIMATE · (•) • • • • ●						BROAD
CLASS	PROJECT	(PEOPLE)				(PATTERN)	

Here's my crappy first draft of the Worthy Goal that was my top priority in 2020:

Stop being CEO of Box of Crayons

I started Box of Crayons almost 20 years ago. To my delight and surprise, it's now a successful learning and development company with 20 employees and a client roster that includes Microsoft, Salesforce, and TELUS. I was an accidental CEO, and while I wasn't terrible at it, I wasn't that great, either. I knew, for the company to continue to flourish, I had to step away.

That's daunting on a number of levels. First, most transitions from Founder to new CEO fail. So, first, how do I ensure I don't screw over Shannon, the CEO-to-be? Second, I have 20 years of identity invested in Box of Crayons. How do I detach from something that is a source of deep meaning and status and purpose for me? Without wanting to go all *L'Étranger* on you, how do I manage through my own existential crisis?

SET A WORTHY GOAL

1 FIND YOUR FOCUS
WRITE A CRAPPY FIRST DRAFT

2 TEST YOUR AMBITION
WRITE AN ACTIVE SECOND DRAFT

3 CLAIM YOUR GOAL
WRITE A STRONG FINAL DRAFT

COMMIT

4 SEE WHERE YOU STAND
FALSE STARTS & MOSQUITOES

5 WEIGH UP THE STATUS QUO
COMFORTS & COSTS

6 WEIGH UP THE JOURNEY
QUALITIES & RISKS

CROSS THE THRESHOLD

7 TAKE SMALL STEPS
HISTORIES, EXPERIMENTS & PRACTICES

8 REMEMBER YOUR BEST SELF
THIS/NOT THAT

9 DON'T TRAVEL ALONE
BUILD THE BAND

HOW TO BEGIN

IN THIS CHAPTER

THE THREE TESTS FOR A WORTHY GOAL

2 TEST YOUR AMBITION

A fine start

You've taken a brave stab at your Worthy Goal with your crappy first draft. It might be tempting to stop now, because it's already a big step forward to have something written down and declared. But don't stop here.

Don't.

Stop.

Here.

It's time to strengthen and fine-tune your draft by testing and triangulating this ambition.

Here are three tests to work through. You don't have to "pass" all or indeed any of the tests. You're just collecting feedback or information. But it's useful to run your draft Worthy Goal through these tests to see what data you gather.

The Spouse-ish Test
(particularly good for testing Thrilling)

If you're lucky, you have a singular person in your life who knows you better than anyone. They're Spouse-ish. It might be a sibling, a BFF, a life partner, a coach, someone who's part of a mastermind group; they could even be your actual spouse.

Whoever it is for you, they've been around you long enough to have heard your stories (a bunch of times), know your dreams, understand your frustrations, and see your patterns. They know your ebb and flow. They still laugh at your jokes (well, some of them), and they have your back.

Go tell your Spouse-ish person your Worthy Goal, and clock their reaction. It's likely to be a variant of these three:

1 Yes! "That's wonderful! Pursue it with gusto!"
2 YES!! "That's great. But seriously: stop talking about it and go and do it. You're driving me nuts."
3 No! "That's ridiculous. Do not do this, I implore you."

I've heard them all at different times. Marcella is my wife and also my Spouse-ish person. I love it when she's excited about an idea. I love it slightly less, but actually appreciate it a little more, when she offers up a no-sugar-coating critique with a 2 or 3 response.

Bear in mind, your Spouse-ish person isn't speaking the truth or issuing a command. You don't need to agree with what they're saying or follow their direction. They're sharing an alternative, insider point of view, a mirror that helps you understand your own level of excitement and commitment. In short: both deeply helpful and also not the truth. For instance, I've had Marcella go hard on Response 3 to a project I've suggested... and I've done it anyway. ←

The FOSO Test (particularly good for testing Important)

I've found it can be helpful to test any Worthy Goal by making explicit its connection to a bigger win that goes beyond my own personal gratification. The bluntest way of doing that is to simply ask, "Why?" But actually, I find "Why?" a pretty hard question to answer. I end up spouting sweeping, self-justifying generalizations that I don't quite believe myself.

Sometimes it's worked out. Sometimes, not so much. Getting clear on the commitment was what mattered.

A more nuanced way to reach the same destination is to see if I can complete this phrase that I add on to the Worthy Goal: "for the sake of..." (which, to make it sound like a cool and upcoming neighbourhood in Brooklyn, I've called FOSO). When I think of some of the Worthy Goals I've achieved, I've been able to offer up a strong answer to the question "Why?" For the *End Malaria* book I created and edited in 2011, it was "for the sake of saving lives" (it raised $400k for Malaria No More). For both *The Coaching Habit* and Box of Crayons, it was "for the sake of un-weirding/making more accessible the idea of coaching." This book too has a "for the sake of": "enabling people to be a force for change."

On the other side of the equation, when I think of most of the projects I've started that have run out of steam and never really got off the ground, the answer to "for the sake of" has been elusive.

Be skeptical about this. "Survivor bias" means that we post-rationalize the quality of the things that work, conveniently forgetting times we've done the same and the project hasn't panned out.

The Goldilocks Zone Test
(particularly good for testing Daunting)

You know the story of Goldilocks, of course: beds, porridge, bears. It all ends well enough (unless you believe in bear property rights, but whatever).

In astronomy, they've taken the essence of the story and defined a Goldilocks Zone, that part of space near a star where water on a planet remains liquid. Too close to the star and the liquid's been boiled off; too far away from the star and it's frozen. But liquid water... that's one of the precursors of life. As we look for exoplanets in deep space, those in the Goldilocks Zone are particularly intriguing.

For your Worthy Goal, you're looking for your own Goldilocks Zone. You're gauging its doability. Does it have the right scope, the right weight? Too small and granular ("I want to go to bed by 10 p.m.") is unlikely to be suitably Thrilling, Important, and Daunting. Too big ("I want to solve racism") is too abstractly aspirational. Does it have a "just right" feel to it? Locating your Worthy Goal in the Goldilocks Zone is the way to ensure it has the right amount of heft.

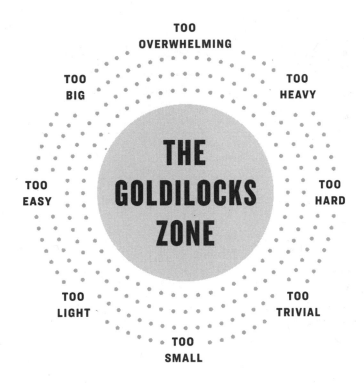

RUN THROUGH THE THREE TESTS

These tests are there to help you get different perspectives on your draft by testing the three dimensions: Thrilling, Important, and Daunting.

How long will this take? Probably 10+ minutes.

Spouse-ish (Thrilling)

When you float your Worthy Goal past your Spouse-ish person, what do you hear? What does that tell you? Where do you agree? Where do you disagree?

_____

_____

_____

_____

_____

_____

FOSO (Important)

When you add and complete the phrase "for the sake of..." to your Worthy Goal, what do you notice? Does it feel connected to an even bigger purpose? Do you believe it,

EXERCISE

or is it spin? What's becoming clear about your Worthy
Goal's possible Importance?

_____

_____

_____

_____

Goldilocks Zone (Daunting)

When you weigh this up, does it feel it's about right?
Not too big to be impossible, not too vague to be un-pin-
downable? Not too hot to burn off your ambition? Not
so cold as to freeze it? Does it have the right heft?

_____

_____

_____

_____

_____

Here's what it looked like for me when I applied the three tests to my own Worthy Goals.

First draft:
Create a new, top-notch podcast

Here's how this crappy first draft stacks up against the three tests:

Spouse-ish (Thrilling): Marcella was supportive. "You like talking to new people, and you're good at it. This makes sense to me." That was nice to hear. Her enthusiasm is a big boost to my own.

FOSO (Important): To launch a new, top-notch podcast for the sake of . . . finding new voices, making wisdom accessible, helping people love books. Yes, I've got reasons that are heartfelt about how this project can give more to the world than it takes. Creating stages where new and different voices can be heard matters. But I'm not sure I've made the connection yet. My justifications feel a little . . . intellectual rather than visceral. So perhaps more work to do here.

Goldilocks Zone (Daunting): Hmm, this is interesting. "Launching a podcast" doesn't feel daunting. I've done a bunch of podcasts already. "Top-notch" ups the ante, but still isn't quite right. There's work for me to do on this part of the Worthy Goal.

EXAMPLE

First draft:
Stop being CEO of Box of Crayons

And here's how this crappy first draft measured against the tests:

Spouse-ish (Thrilling): Marcella was very excited at the idea. Some of it's her own agenda (helpful to remember), but she also reminded me of more carefree days when I didn't have the weight of being CEO.

FOSO (Important): Box of Crayons is a purpose-driven business. The mission is to help organizations move from advice-driven to curiosity-led action... but the "for the sake of" is "helping to bring humanity to the workplace." I'm very committed to the success of this mission. But if I stay on as CEO, I don't have the skills or the focus to grow and scale the company, and that will fatally compromise our dreams to have the impact we want.

But that's not all. A second FOSO is that I'm committed to learning about, and role-modelling, how to give up power: finding ways to invite in others who are more typically excluded from opportunities. This goal is very much about that commitment.

Goldilocks Zone (Daunting): Oh, *soooo* daunting. The thought of stepping away from a position I've been in for nigh on 20 years is pretty scary. Who am I when I'm not the founder of Box of Crayons? That said, it doesn't feel as though it's impossible. It's not some pipe dream.

Verbing

After you run your first draft through the three tests, it's time to write an active second draft of your Worthy Goal.

As well as making any adjustments you've gleaned from the Spouse-ish, FOSO, and Goldilocks tests, I've got one other challenge: I want you to start this next draft with a verb.

By beginning your Worthy Goal with a verb, you're committing to action. Defining the outcome is deeply helpful: it points you in the right direction and it fires you up. That's why we're spending so much time on it now. But it's by working the process that you make progress. It's by *doing* the hard things that we unlock our greatness.

Yes, I've verbed the noun. It's a grammatical crime.

Creating your second draft with a verb makes it an active draft. There's a list of verbs you can draw upon on the next page.

WRITE AN ACTIVE SECOND DRAFT OF YOUR WORTHY GOAL

Adjust your Worthy Goal based on the three tests, and your verb of choice.

How long will this take? Probably 10 + minutes.

_____

_____

EXERCISE

_____

_____

_____

_____

_____

Verbs for your active draft

BEGIN. _Set up._ **INITIATE.** _Dismantle._ **LAUNCH.** _Dare._ **HIRE.** _Start._ **FINISH.** _Create._ **BREAK.** _Fire._ **PRODUCE.** _Change._ **REINVENT.** _Summon._ **ASK FOR.** _Reach out._ **CHALLENGE.** _Marry._ **ABDICATE.** _Protest._ **IMPROVE.** _Record._ **WORK OUT.** _Collaborate with._ **BUILD.** _Defenestrate._ **REFRAME.** _Plant._ **TRANSFORM.** _Pursue._ **DISRUPT.** _Connect with._ **ENGAGE.** _Bring together._ **HARVEST.** _Seize._ **STUDY.** _Follow._ **TEACH.** **RE-ENGAGE.** _Instigate._ **VENTURE.** _Unleash._ **PROVIDE.** _Rearrange._ **POST.** _Sort out._ **KICKSTART.** _Write._ **CONFRONT.** **COMMIT TO.** _Toss out._ **INVITE.** _Defy._ **LEAD.** _Join._ **FREE.** _Organize._ **RETURN TO.** _Reinitiate._ **GENERATE.** _Construct._ **CONNECT TO.** _Partner with._ **LET GO OF.** _Liberate._ **INVITE.** _Remove._ **WORK ON.** _Found._ **ENROL IN.** _Love._

You can "Give a Verb, Take a Verb" at HowToBegin.com. If this list doesn't do it for you, you'll find an expanded list there.

Here are my active second drafts.

First draft:
Create a new, top-notch podcast

I'm trying to fine-tune my original goal of creating a top-notch podcast. It fell a little short in the "Daunting" category. It also needed a more compelling verb. Bearing all that in mind, I came up with this as my second crack at it:

Second draft:
Launch a new, professional-grade podcast

"Launch" is a much more useful verb for me, as it shifts the focus to getting it out into the world, not just creating something. "Professional-grade" is more specific. "Top-notch" is a bit slippery, and I could post-rationalize pretty much anything I do against that. "Professional" has a much clearer edge.

EXAMPLE

First draft:
Stop being CEO of Box of Crayons

"Stop being CEO" named what was happening, but it was too small a statement. It wasn't just me stepping away from the role. It was also finding a new CEO and having them successfully take over the role.

Second draft:
Manage the transition out of the CEO role

This gets much closer to the real challenge. After all, it's easy enough to stop being CEO. You just … stop. But figuring out the transition? That's where the hard work really is, and the difference between success and failure.

SET A WORTHY GOAL

1 FIND YOUR FOCUS
WRITE A CRAPPY FIRST DRAFT

2 TEST YOUR AMBITION
WRITE AN ACTIVE SECOND DRAFT

3 CLAIM YOUR GOAL
WRITE A STRONG FINAL DRAFT

COMMIT

4 SEE WHERE YOU STAND
FALSE STARTS & MOSQUITOES

5 WEIGH UP THE STATUS QUO
COMFORTS & COSTS

6 WEIGH UP THE JOURNEY
QUALITIES & RISKS

CROSS THE THRESHOLD

7 TAKE SMALL STEPS
HISTORIES, EXPERIMENTS & PRACTICES

8 REMEMBER YOUR BEST SELF
THIS/NOT THAT

9 DON'T TRAVEL ALONE
BUILD THE BAND

HOW TO BEGIN

IN THIS CHAPTER

**TIGHTEN AND
STRENGTHEN YOUR
WORTHY GOAL**

3 CLAIM YOUR GOAL

The Voting Test

You're about to give your Worthy Goal one final working over to get it as close as possible to a final draft that is genuinely Thrilling, Important, and Daunting. After a final edit, you'll be ready to declare victory (or at least "Good enough!" which is often the same thing).

Here's how you take stock of where you are: the Voting Test.

Let's go back to our three core criteria: Thrilling, Important, and Daunting. Against each of those, rate the current expression of your Worthy Goal out of 7.

RATE YOUR CURRENT WORTHY GOAL DRAFT

Against each of the three core criteria, rate the current expression of your Worthy Goal out of 7. This will give you a total out of 21—21 being straight 7s. Don't plump up the result: this is just for you. You're not trying to impress anyone with your score. You're just figuring how close you are to the mark.

How long will this take? Probably about five minutes.

Thrilling: / 7
_____

Because:
_____

_____

Important: / 7
_____

Because:
_____

_____

Daunting: / 7
_____

Because:
_____

_____

Total: / 21

My hypothesis (and this is why it's called the Voting Test) is that if the score is not 18 or higher, the Worthy Goal is not yet ready. I don't have any science behind this, but when I've facilitated people through this process, this calibration is a key step towards getting closer to a really powerful Worthy Goal.

Here's how I'm rating my current drafts.

Second draft: Launch a new, professional-grade podcast

Thrilling: 4 / 7
I've done podcasts before, so it doesn't quite have the edge of the new and exciting.

Important: 5 / 7
My vision for this podcast is that it's a powerful way to spread ideas, and to find new voices and points of view to share with the world.

Daunting: 5 / 7
"Professional-grade" definitely ups the ante from "top-notch." But ... to be honest, I'm not quite sure what that phrase means either. I kind of get it ... but I don't know how to measure it yet. So it hasn't landed for me. But it's getting closer.

Total: 14 / 21

EXAMPLE

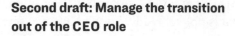

Second draft: Manage the transition out of the CEO role

Thrilling: 4 / 7

Honestly, it depends on what side of the bed I get out of. Sometimes it's a 1, sometimes it's a 7! On balance, though, I'm more excited about the thought of not being CEO than I am afraid of it. But "manage the transition" is not a thrilling phrase for me. So, let's go with 4.

Important: 7 / 7

It's imperative that Box of Crayons has a new CEO if it's going to scale, thrive, and have the impact it might. It's a little disappointing to admit, but I don't have the skills or the focus to make it happen if I stay on as CEO.

Daunting: 6 / 7

There are two levels here for me. On the one hand, I have no idea how to do this. I've heard lots of horror stories. On the other hand, I also know that there are people who do know how to do this, people I can call on. That would make it a 4 or 5. The next level is about how hard it will be for me to actually do it. That's a clear 7. So let's say 6 is the middle ground.

Total: 17–20 / 21

EXAMPLE

Add one word

One of my favourite restaurants in Toronto is the Salad King. They have a "heat scale," which goes from 1 chili (mild) to 3 (medium) all the way to 20 (nuts). In my experience one word can take you further up the chili scale of your Worthy Goal. You don't need to top out the Scoville scale: *way* too much sweat and pain. But you do want a little more heat.

The Voting Test helps you reset how you're feeling about your Worthy Goal. It helps you step outside the subjective experience of wrestling with the details, and gives you a more clinical (but still personal) reading against the three essential criteria. No matter your score—even if, as I saw one person calculate, you're at 26/21—the final challenge is to see if there's just one word (or short phrase) that, if added, would tighten the power and focus of your Worthy Goal.

There's no magic, generic word, of course. But there are six different axes you might consider where there's an opportunity to fine-tune that current draft. You'll see it's not always about bigger and bolder and broader. In fact, the power is often in setting more specific parameters. Setting limits can light the fuse.

Commitment: Be more specific about how much you're willing to give. This can be time, energy, or money. It can also be the spirit in which you give.

Reach: Be more specific about how wide or narrow you'd like to go. It can be about the size of your audience, and it can also be about your geographic reach.

Time: Be more specific about how long this will take or when you'd like it to reach a certain stage.

Scope: Be clear about how narrow or expansive this might be. It can help put an end point on what you're thinking.

Standard: Be more specific about the quality you'd like to deliver. This is often an internal, subjective measure.

Outcome: Be more specific about your desired outcome. This is most often an external, objective measure.

Neil Pasricha's outstanding *3 Books* podcast releases its episodes on these markers. My newsletter does the same. Sign up at MBS.works.

There's a list below that will get you started. As you think about your third and final draft, don't overload it. This isn't the Adjective Buffet. Pick one word or phrase that will make this Worthy Goal of yours zing!

Add one word/phrase to intensify your Worthy Goal

Commitment: Full-time. Four hours a week. Dedicated. Every waking moment. With a team. Willingly. Joyfully. All in.

Reach: Local. Globally. Worldwide. 1,000 true fans. 10 million fans.

Time: By tomorrow. By March. Within six weeks. By the end of the year. By 2050. Before I die.

Scope: One-off. Annually. A series. A franchise. Every full moon and new moon. Regularly.

Standard: Professional. Elite. Completed. Extraordinary. Good enough. Competent. Graciously. Handmade. Evolving. Generously. Lovingly. Committed.

Outcome: Profitable. Lucrative. Sustainable. Launched. Approved. Recognized. Helpful. Freeing. Top 3 percent. Bestseller. Classic. Transformative. Evergreen.

You can "Give a Word, Take a Word" at HowToBegin.com. If this list doesn't do it for you, you'll find an expanded list there.

WRITE A STRONG FINAL DRAFT

You've done brilliantly to get here. Using all you've learned, having run the Voting Test, and bearing in mind the option of adding one word (or short phrase), you will now take a crack at writing your best strong final draft.

How long will this take? Probably anywhere from 1 to 10+ minutes.

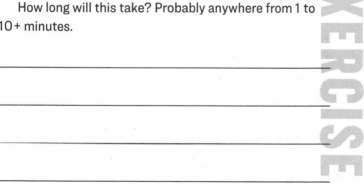

Here are my final drafts.

Second draft: Launch a new, professional-grade podcast

I ended up writing and rewriting this Worthy Goal. At one stage it expanded to be a podcast media company with a family of different podcasts. Then it shrank again.

I experimented with all sorts of adjectives, but was finally inspired when I read a provocative article which posited that being in the top 5 percent (of anything) isn't as hard as it sounds. With some research I discovered that being in the top 3 percent of podcasts means 10,000 downloads per episode within a month of release. I like that specificity. I also like what it implies, in terms of production quality, distribution, advertising, the team behind it, and so on. It sets a completely different standard from any podcast project I've done before.

Final draft: Launch a new podcast that is in the top 3 percent of all podcasts within 12 months

This Worthy Goal is now at 19/21.
Thrilling: 6. Important: 6. Daunting: 7.

EXAMPLE

Second draft: Manage the transition out of the CEO role

This is still a bit bloodless as a Worthy Goal. It might even be a backwards step from my first draft. In wrestling with the final draft, I connected deeply to my FOSO Test: *be someone who gives up power, rather than holds on to it.* That was the breakthrough I needed. It really firmed up the Important part, and in fact made the Thrilling a stronger 7 too.

Final draft: Role-model a gracious, generous, and trusting transfer of power

This is now a rock-solid 21/21.
Thrilling: 7. Important: 7. Daunting: 7.

Good enough? That's good enough

You may well have dropped the proverbial Worthy Goal mic and left the building after the last exercise. That's how it happened for me, particularly as I worked through my example about the CEO transition, and I'd be thrilled if it happened that way for you too.

But maybe you're thinking: "It's close, it's interesting, but it's still not *quite* there." Or perhaps adding that word or phrase made it a little too grandiose. It sounds amazing, but perhaps it's now so daunting it feels impossible and actually demotivating.

BUT TO GROW UP
COSTS THE EARTH, THE
EARTH. IT MEANS YOU
TAKE RESPONSIBILITY
FOR THE TIME YOU
TAKE UP.

MAYA ANGELOU

You've got a choice now: press on or linger here a little longer to refine your Worthy Goal. In order to do that, you need to know what standard you're working towards. After all the work you've put in, it may sound odd to remind you of the standard we're looking for. "Perfection," whatever that actually is, is not it. Seeking "perfection" just runs the risk of leaving you becalmed. "Perfection" is just misery dressed up in fancy clothes.

We actually want "good enough." "Good enough" can be a tricky standard to hold, mostly because it *sounds* very close to "not good at all." But "good enough" means it's over the line, it's in the light, it's made the cut. Making the call requires something of a gut feel now. Use the list of standards on the next page to gauge where you are with your Worthy Goal.

If you find you need to spend more time working on the Worthy Goal, excellent. Keep at it. Go through the process again. Give yourself time. Be gentle, but press on. Find a friend or a coach or a teacher or a friendly stranger in a bar, and have them help you go through the How to Begin process. You're *this close* to getting it right, so don't stop now.

And if you're ready to move on, take a short break. Because in the next section you'll decide to Commit. And that begins with a slightly awkward reality check.

Making the call

The next stage of the How to Begin process is: Commit. How do you know if you're ready?

You're ready and raring to go if your Worthy Goal final draft is...

- Clear as a bell
- Strong like titanium
- Simplicity on the other side of complexity
- "Hell yes!"
- Undeniable
- Irresistible
- Going all in

You're also great to proceed if your Worthy Goal final draft is...

- Good enough
- Solid
- Worth a go
- There's enough there there
- "That works"
- Essentially correct

A particular favourite of mine.

COMMIT

YOU INHALE, YOU EXHALE.

YOU'RE GROUNDED,

CONFIDENT, AND CLEAR.

READY TO COMMIT.

Take a breath

If you watch anyone on the verge of starting something that matters, you'll see them settle into the moment by taking a deep breath in... and exhaling. That out-breath marks clarity and commitment. The Olympic swimmer as they step up onto the block and prepare for the gun. The speaker in the wings before they're called out onto the stage. The yoga student settling into the pose. The cursor hovering over the Submit button onscreen, your finger on the mouse. It's the body rolling up its metaphorical sleeves and saying: *OK. It's time. Let's do this thing.*

In this section, we're slowing down a little, expanding, and lingering in this moment. You've defined your Worthy Goal, and that's exciting. Part of you is raring to go. This is the moment where you settle into *your* commitment.

1 **See where you stand** right now. That's going to take a little forensic accounting—I'm deliberately choosing a phrase that's a bit clinical—looking into both the past and the here and now to see what's going on.

2 **Weigh up the status quo.** Until you understand your commitment to how things are right now and why you *don't* want to start your Worthy Goal—a commitment that has deeper roots than you realize—it's almost impossible to prise yourself free.

3 **Weigh up the journey** ahead of you as you commit to your Worthy Goal. There are pros and cons, prizes and punishments to deciding to cross the threshold. You need to know what they are.

SET A WORTHY GOAL

1 FIND YOUR FOCUS
WRITE A CRAPPY FIRST DRAFT

2 TEST YOUR AMBITION
WRITE AN ACTIVE SECOND DRAFT

3 CLAIM YOUR GOAL
WRITE A STRONG FINAL DRAFT

COMMIT

4 SEE WHERE YOU STAND
FALSE STARTS & MOSQUITOES

5 WEIGH UP THE STATUS QUO
COMFORTS & COSTS

6 WEIGH UP THE JOURNEY
QUALITIES & RISKS

CROSS THE THRESHOLD

7 TAKE SMALL STEPS
HISTORIES, EXPERIMENTS & PRACTICES

8 REMEMBER YOUR BEST SELF
THIS/NOT THAT

9 DON'T TRAVEL ALONE
BUILD THE BAND

IN THIS CHAPTER

TRANSCEND YOUR FALSE STARTS

4 SEE WHERE YOU STAND

Be present

Dave Snowden's a Philosopher King in the space of complexity-meets-decision-making-and-strategy. He's Welsh, which means he can get away with naming his theory Cynefin, a word that few people know how to pronounce and fewer know how to define. Like so many of my favourite thinkers, he's brilliant and a bit prickly.

Back in October 2020 Dave tweeted:

Ken'EV-in, maybe. It means "habitat" but in a way that incorporates multiple meanings of habitat.

If you want to make any real difference then stop making lists of idealised qualities of how things should be—they will always end up as anodyne platitudes—focus on understanding and critically ACTING in the present to start shifting things in a better direction.

"Understanding the present." It's difficult, perhaps impossible, to achieve your Worthy Goal if you don't know where you're starting from. There's enormous benefit in taking the time to close-read who you are now and what your patterns and commitments are before you set out.

Be forewarned: this part of the How to Begin process is challenging and provocative. It asks you to examine what *isn't* going so well. It's a confession of past and present struggles. That means you'll be walking a fine line. It's not about making you feel bad and "less than," even though I know I'm setting you up with a perfect opportunity to beat yourself up. I also don't want you to skip through this and not do this essential work. So as you work through the next two steps, hold in balance these contradictory directions from me: be unflinching and clear-eyed and look for the truth, and be kind to yourself as you do so.

You'll start by looking at your False Starts: times when you made a half-hearted and/or ill-fated attempt at something like your Worthy Goal.

You've been here before

You have almost certainly declared an intention to do something that matters before, something that's in some way Thrilling, Important, and Daunting. It might have shown up, along with a glass of champagne, at midnight on December 31. It might have appeared at some other time, a moment when inspiration and ambition commingled. A tug on your sleeve, nudging you: *Dream big. Dare bravely. Pursue boldly. Commit.*

And commonly enough, not every time but likely the majority of times, you made little or no progress on it. You were becalmed, undone by some combination of: you didn't know where to start; you didn't know who to ask; you were denied access to resources and support; you made a few False Starts and lost heart; you were told you weren't the right person; you didn't trust the plan; you didn't master the skill immediately; you ran out of puff; you got ⟵ distracted; you put it away "for now"; you were told to stop.

If this is you, you're in excellent company. I and the rest of humanity are waving hello.

What makes that feel worse is that you—yes, you—most likely know a bit about change and personal growth. You've read some books, seen TED Talks, followed influencers, and subscribed to podcasts and newsletters. Maybe hired a coach. Perhaps even trained to be a coach. "What's *wrong* with me," you might think, "that I can't figure this out?"

Don't do the usual and sweep these False Starts under the rug or conveniently "forget" about them. Instead, bring the stories out of the shadows and take a look. "Where," you can ask yourself, "have I seen something like this before?" Note all the versions and close relations to your Worthy Goal that you dabbled in or flirted with, versions that trailed off or never really got going; were shelved or put away in the drawer;

were mocked or lost their mojo; were scaled down and then down again to nothing.

Acknowledge those times when you were disheartened, discouraged, discombobulated, distracted, and stuck.

ACKNOWLEDGE YOUR FALSE STARTS

List False Starts on projects similar to the one you've articulated as your Worthy Goal. You'll find a diminishing return spending too much time here. I think it's helpful if you've captured more than two and fewer than six False Starts. It's enough to show you some patterns.

If you have nothing to note, that's fine as well. It might well be that your Worthy Goal is brand new territory and in a completely different class from anything you've ever attempted before. But do take a good hard look around before you decide for sure there's nothing here.

How long will this take? Probably 10+ minutes.

EXERCISE

_____

_____

_____

_____

_____

I've been in plenty of cul-de-sacs myself, dead ends where I had to reverse out and find a new way forward.

Launch a new podcast that is in the top 3 percent of all podcasts within 12 months

I've got a juicy and somewhat embarrassing history of False Starts when it comes to podcasts. I've previously dabbled with six podcasts, one of which was substantial (*The Great Work Podcast*, 350 episodes); and five others that weren't (*Performance Management Stories*, *The Coaching Habit*, *Five Questions with MBS*, *Best of MBS*, and *We Will Get Through This*).

If I look out beyond just "podcasts," I notice False Starts dealing with the idea of "top 3 percent," including assorted forays into online advertising that cost a lot and delivered little; a few attempted partnerships that involved a lot of talking and no action . . . and the list carries on.

EXAMPLE

Role-model a gracious, generous, and trusting transfer of power

I've never given up being a CEO before, so I don't have anything exactly analogous to that. But this goal is about a trusting transfer of power, and it turns out I can think of numerous times I've done that poorly in the past.

As I reflect, I see two main patterns in my past behaviour. One is "dump and run": employ magic thinking and hope that the person can somehow read my mind and my heart, knows what I want, and will succeed if I sketch a loose brief and disappear from sight. I've been #LearningNotLearning about this for many years.

The other pattern is almost the opposite: micromanaging people. Nominally give over power, but hold on to a few things like, say, all the decision-making power. In other words, do a fake power transfer, which is really a dump of all the things I don't want to do, while holding on to all the cool bits and pieces.

That's the first part of forensic accounting done. Don't get too comfortable, though. The next part, Notice the Mosquitoes, will be provocative... and also, probably, incredibly freeing.

EXAMPLE

Notice the Mosquitoes

My grandmother, my dad's mum, was Maida Euphemia Kerr Stanier (née Burnett), and she was the first writer I knew. She was a classics scholar and lived in Oxford, and wrote books for adults and children alike. She was also the gossip columnist for the local paper, and her *nom de plume* was Culex, the Latin word for mosquito. I like the idea of her buzzing around, drawing a little blood here and a little blood there...

Which is my middle name. That's right: Michael Burnett Bungay Stanier.

Mosquitoes are both tiny and mighty. Anita Roddick, founder of the Body Shop, famously said, "If you think you're too small to have an impact, try going to bed with a mosquito in the room." The 200 million or more people who contract malaria every year would agree.

Your Worthy Goal comes with a cloud of its own Mosquitoes. These Mosquitoes are all the things you're currently doing and not doing—secular sins of commission and of omission—that are contrary to this Worthy Goal you've set for yourself. You'll find they're numerous. Some are tiny, others more significant. No single Mosquito is fatal in and of itself, but together they irritate you, weaken you, slow you down, and distract you from your Worthy Goal.

For this part of the process, you will own up to all your Mosquitoes. It will be awkward. It was probably a little embarrassing to list those False Starts a few minutes ago, but at least they're historical. Listing your Mosquitoes will be worse. This is you confessing, owning up to the ways you're actively undermining your Worthy Goal, colluding against your own ambitions, scuttling your dreams.

YOU'LL HAVE A REACTION TO THIS

JUST ABOUT

NOW

You'll want to tell me about the assorted things you're doing that *are* moving you towards that Worthy Goal. I salute them. I salute you. But—to be blunt—I don't care about what you're doing that's *good* right now. At this point, I'm just interested in your Mosquitoes.

NOTICE YOUR MOSQUITOES

Write down the things you're currently doing and not doing that are not leading towards your Worthy Goal. Actions and non-actions, big and small. Make them tangible and real.

Sometimes it can be a bit slow to get going; that first five minutes will help give you momentum, and you can carry on if it feels helpful. I've found that once I get going, the confessions start to flow. If you're running out of things to write down, ask yourself, "And what else?"

How long will this take? Probably 10+ minutes.

Actions	Non-Actions

EXERCISE

Here's my swarm.

Launch a new podcast that is in the top 3 percent of all podcasts within 12 months

Things I'm doing that are contrary to this goal include: investing in a consultant then ignoring her recommendations; setting a standard then immediately downgrading the ambition of the podcast to make it smaller; starting another, unrelated podcast that I can do in my usual small-scale way; being timid about the guests I'm inviting to the unrelated podcast; buying expensive podcast equipment then not learning how to set it up properly. Refusing to figure out the marketing...

Things I'm not doing are even more numerous. They include: not creating a vision for the podcast; not setting a budget (time or money); not listening to other "role model" podcasts; not hiring a professional podcasting agency; not attending a podcasting conference; not learning about podcast marketing; not calling myself a podcast host; not exploring distribution partnerships...

EXAMPLE

Role-model a gracious, generous, and trusting transfer of power

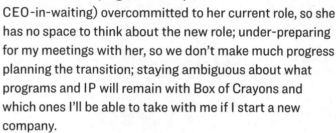

Things I'm doing contrary to my Worthy Goal include: keeping Shannon (the CEO-in-waiting) overcommitted to her current role, so she has no space to think about the new role; under-preparing for my meetings with her, so we don't make much progress planning the transition; staying ambiguous about what programs and IP will remain with Box of Crayons and which ones I'll be able to take with me if I start a new company.

Things I'm not doing include: not establishing a formal transfer date; not setting up a decision-making hierarchy; not defining the role of CEO for my successor; not distinguishing between the things I want to give up and the things I want to keep; not preparing a "life after Box of Crayons."

Be kind to yourself: Reset and recovery

It can be arduous to list all those actions, past and present, that are contrary to your Worthy Goal. It can quickly become the excuse-you-really-didn't-need to beat yourself up.

You can chastise yourself for False Starts: "I stumbled forward briefly, then fell down. Repeatedly." Mosquitoes—how you're currently conspiring against

> # COMPASSION IS THE PRIMARY EXPERIENCE... OUT OF WHICH EMERGES THE GENIUS AND GENEROSITY OF THE IMAGINATION.
> NICK CAVE

your own ambition—can spark an even harsher interior monologue. Here's what it sounds like in my head: "What the hell is WRONG with you, Michael? You're an adult! You're educated; heck, you're a Rhodes Scholar! And you can't do this? You seem to be without smarts, focus, discipline, or backbone. I'm not exactly sure what laurels you're resting on, but you're sure taking a long nap here. Good grief! How did you con whoever you've conned to get here? You're a grab bag of excuses wrapped up in an overly colourful shirt."

You might have your own version of this Inner Critic or Gremlin, as it's sometimes called. Let's nip it in the bud. Spending time beating yourself up only makes your pursuit of a Worthy Goal harder. Here are two ways you can choose to shift the energy, and snatch victory from the jaws of defeat.

Hip hop & classical

When Outkast sang, "Now throw ya hands in the air/ And wave 'em like ya just don't care," they were on to something that goes beyond dancing to old-school hip hop. Ros and Ben Zander, co-authors of *The Art of Possibility*, took the dancing one step further. They suggest that when things go wrong, you throw your hands up in the air and say, "How fascinating!"

Ben Zander has a British accent, so obviously it always sounds better when he says it. But no matter your accent, it's one of those simple-but-genius moves. It takes you into a place of curiosity. It encourages you to see it as feedback, not failure. It invites you to hold things more lightly. It says, "Be kind to yourself." It hints that this too will pass. From a place of "How fascinating!" you can learn and you can let go.

That's a good temporary fix, and you should use it with regular abandon in all sorts of circumstances. But there's a deeper, more structural reason why you can be kinder to yourself about the False Starts and Mosquitoes. It turns out that they're an absolutely necessary part of this adventure.

Resistance is ~~futile~~ celebrated

You may have heard about the Hero's Journey. It's one model for the narrative of "we unlock our greatness by doing the hard things." The path, broadly speaking,

takes you across the threshold and into the unknown to defeat the monster, claim the prize, and journey back to the light, changed and bringing change.

However, the Hero's Journey doesn't start by simply opening the front door, stepping over the threshold, and striding down the path towards success. That's far too neat and tidy, and crucially overlooks one step that's non-negotiable. When the hero first hears the call, they refuse the call.

THEY REFUSE THE CALL! I'm shouting, because I want you to register this as an essential part of the process.

You can probably feel this tension now. When you define your Worthy Goal with its entwined ambitions—for you and for the world—one part of you is thrilled by the idea. Changing things up, leaving some things behind, making a difference, becoming different. Bring it on!

But there's another part, a bigger part than you might realize, that hates the idea. It's there in your body. Maybe your shoulders are drifting upwards. Maybe you're breathing a little shallowly. Maybe, like me, you're jiggling your leg.

It's not the only story, and there's been some useful feminist criticism of this model in recent years. Elizabeth Lesser's book *Cassandra Speaks* is a helpful counter-narrative.

But those apparent backward steps you've listed can be recast in a wonderful way. No longer are they some sign of moral failing and lack of character. Rather, they're evidence that you're on a path that matters. That Worthy Goal really *is* something worth pursuing. Reluctance and hesitation are an inevitable consequence of taking on something that's Thrilling, Important, and Daunting.

All those times it's difficult, when you notice the resistance, when you seem to be avoiding the adventure that's unfolding in front of you ... those aren't moments of failure, those are moments of *confirmation*.

Hope is not a strategy

You've tallied your behaviours, past and present, noticed your resistance and the ways you currently collude against your own ambition. But just hoping you can get going on your Worthy Goal isn't going to cut it. How do you actually commit? By weighing up the consequences of *not* pursuing your Worthy Goal.

SET A WORTHY GOAL

1 FIND YOUR FOCUS
WRITE A CRAPPY FIRST DRAFT

2 TEST YOUR AMBITION
WRITE AN ACTIVE SECOND DRAFT

3 CLAIM YOUR GOAL
WRITE A STRONG FINAL DRAFT

COMMIT

4 SEE WHERE YOU STAND
FALSE STARTS & MOSQUITOES

5 WEIGH UP THE STATUS QUO
COMFORTS & COSTS

6 WEIGH UP THE JOURNEY
QUALITIES & RISKS

CROSS THE THRESHOLD

7 TAKE SMALL STEPS
HISTORIES, EXPERIMENTS & PRACTICES

8 REMEMBER YOUR BEST SELF
THIS/NOT THAT

9 DON'T TRAVEL ALONE
BUILD THE BAND

IN THIS CHAPTER

NAME THE PRIZES &
PUNISHMENTS
BETWEEN YOU AND
YOUR WORTHY GOAL

5 WEIGH UP THE STATUS QUO

We ♥ the status quo

One of my favourite Gary Larson cartoons shows a moose slumped in a ratty armchair watching the television, can of beer in hand, paunch on display, the acme of stuck-in-a-rut-ness. His moose wife, hair in curlers, stands with her hand over the phone's handset: "It's the call of the wild."

What if, like our moose friend, you choose not to answer the call? Imagine *not* taking on this Worthy Goal. Imagine that the Mosquitoes keep biting. Imagine if you let this opportunity slide past.

It can feel like a sign of weakness or a betrayal somehow to bring that possibility to the surface. But answering it is absolutely essential for progress. There *are* very tangible reasons—Prizes—for not taking on the Worthy Goal. We're far more committed to the status quo than we realize. Until you fully understand this commitment, promises that run deep and are often unspoken and unrecognized, it's hard to shift that allegiance. Equally, there are very tangible consequences—Punishments—for stepping away from this opportunity. Until you understand the cost to you and others for not taking on your Worthy Goal, you may never be pulled forward to commit.

In weighing up the status quo, you'll balance out the Prizes & Punishments of not taking on your Worthy Goal. It's in this weighing up that your choice to follow through or not will become clear.

This is a bit brain-twisty. It's like a double negative. Here's the simplest way I can put it: the Punishments of not doing something = the Prizes of the status quo.

Prizes: Comfort

Broadly speaking, the Prize for not taking on the Worthy Goal is the maintenance of what you've gathered in your life so far. What that looks like is different for each of us, but the underlying themes are the same. You'll maintain comfort, status, authority, privilege, familiarity, and control. You'll protect and keep hidden vulnerabilities and insecurities.

Prizes for not taking on your Worthy Goal might include not disrupting the way others see you or disappointing the expectations they have of you; not having to challenge your own limiting stories about yourself; not stepping out to

A TOUCH OF MADNESS, I THINK, IS ALMOST ALWAYS NECESSARY FOR CONSTRUCTING A DESTINY.

MARGUERITE YOURCENAR

the edges of your experience, competence, and confidence; and finding ways to let yourself off the hook, or play small, or keep being a victim, or stay disengaged, or be cynical.

I've taken to calling these Prizes #WinsNotWins, because while they genuinely do offer something in the immediate moment, they're mostly pyrrhic victories: protecting our egos and others'; playing by others' rules; staying hidden. They're certainly not about unlocking greatness by taking on the hard things.

IDENTIFY THE PRIZES OF THE STATUS QUO

How would you benefit from *not* taking on your Worthy Goal? What would be the "Prizes"? What would be the #WinsNotWins?

I know this is hard, deep work. Give yourself time, and what you'll uncover will be powerful stuff.

How long will this take? Probably 10+ minutes.

EXERCISE

_____

_____

_____

_____

_____

Having made that list, what insights do you have? What patterns do you notice?

_____

_____

_____

_____

_____

Here's why the status quo has a strong pull on me.

Launch a new podcast that is in the top 3 percent of all podcasts within 12 months

If I didn't take this on...

- I'd have time for other projects. I'd be able to keep my options open.

- I could keep dabbling and maintain my "lucky/competent amateur" story.

- I wouldn't risk failing, and exposing my naïveté about podcasting.

- I wouldn't face learning that I don't have much of a fan base.

- I wouldn't put at risk my "successful entrepreneur" tag.

- I wouldn't have to risk hiring new people, and trusting them.

- I can keep my money, rather than risk losing it on this venture.

- I wouldn't have to "sell out" by becoming an "influencer" or having to understand marketing.

- I can keep telling myself that people like Tim Ferriss are different from me, and that I'll never have that success because he's somehow been blessed by the gods.

- I wouldn't have my thinking and beliefs challenged by talking to guests who see the world differently from me.

EXAMPLE

What I notice here

I've got a *lot* of stories that stroke my ego and say I'm just fine as I am ("for a dabbler, you're pretty good"; "you have some fans"; "you know how to be an entrepreneur"). They're largely untested but still precious to me. Keeping these stories alive feels... comforting.

EXAMPLE

Role-model a gracious, generous, and trusting transfer of power

If I didn't take this on...

- I keep the status and rank of being a Founder and a CEO.

- I keep having subordinates who "work for me."

- I continue to benefit from specific technical expertise that I've built up.

- I keep being part of a thriving company with people I love to work with.

- I keep taking credit for the success Box of Crayons is having.

- I get to ensure my legacy in all sorts of small ways, from the values we have in the company to the language we use in marketing.

- I keep control of... so many things!

- I don't have to face what it means to give up power, something I'm not sure I fully understand.

- I don't have to craft a new identity for myself separate from Box of Crayons.

- I don't have to risk finding out that I wasn't able to manage this transition, and that I fell into all the traps that happen in most Founder transitions.

What I notice here

I have a lot of my ego invested in my role as a CEO. But the thing I'm most twitchy about is what it means to give up power. I'm excited about that in theory. In practice... well, I'm not so sure.

Punishments: Costs

You have to see both sides of the equation before you can see how it all adds up. We've done Prizes, and now we have to do something similar with Punishments.

We start by looking at the price paid by *you* should you choose not to Cross the Threshold, take on the Worthy Goal, and have this adventure. At its heart will likely be the extinguishing of future possibilities. You miss a chance to unlock your greatness.

But the price of your not engaging is also paid by others, not just you. If it was only about you, it would be easier to find all sorts of slippery reasons why it's OK for you to pay the price. We can fall back on old stories about being a Victim or a Rescuer or whatever to justify the suffering.

Language from the Karpman Drama Triangle, a powerful tool for understanding how relationships go off the rails, which I teach in *The Coaching Habit*.

Your Worthy Goal is Thrilling, Important, and Daunting. "Important" means that whether you take this on or not affects *others*. You need to account for the way we *all* lose should you not take on your Worthy Goal.

IDENTIFY THE PUNISHMENTS OF THE STATUS QUO

What price would you (and others) pay should you *not* take on your Worthy Goal?

Review some of the notes you made for the FOSO Test (in the "Test Your Ambition" step) as grist for the mill. What you wrote down as "for the sake of..." will likely be part of your answer to this part of the process.

Give yourself time: this is important work.

How long will this take? Probably 10+ minutes.

What's the price being paid ... by you?

EXERCISE

_____

_____

_____

_____

_____

_____

What's the price being paid ... by them (those directly impacted)?

_____

_____

_____

_____

What's the price being paid ... by us (the broader world)?

_____

_____

_____

_____

Having made those lists, what insights do you have? What patterns do you notice?

_____

_____

_____

Here's what I notice about my own Worthy Goals.

 **Launch a new podcast that is in the top 3 percent of all podcasts within 12 months**

If you *didn't* commit to this Worthy Goal, what would the Punishments be? What would be the price being paid?

For me
- I'd be resigned to having hit my peak with *The Coaching Habit*, and being in terminal decline.
- I wouldn't get to meet brilliant authors and thinkers.
- I wouldn't get to master a new area of specialty.
- I'd miss my best idea for being a translator of ideas, for making wisdom accessible.
- I'd spend the rest of my working life dabbling in small-scale projects.
- I'd get firmly taken in by the "lucky amateur" story.
- I wouldn't use my luck and privilege and talents for good.
- I wouldn't practise what I preach.

For them (people who interact directly with the podcast in some way)
- Jobs are not available to work on the podcast, as producers and hosts.

- Opportunities are not available to talk about their books, for authors who are looking to share their best work.

- Opportunities to get exposed to new thinkers and writers are not available, for listeners of the podcast.

For us (the broader world)
- Narrowing of culture: more TikTok, fewer books.

- Fewer role models of people starting new projects and being open to the experience.

What I notice here
The richest vein here is definitely the price being paid by me. The list is starting to feel like a betrayal of some core values I hope I hold. The price being paid by "them" and "us" holds less heat for me. Still, it's helpful to see them there and get clearer about the bigger "why" behind my work.

Role-model a gracious, generous, and trusting transfer of power

If you *didn't* commit to this Worthy Goal, what would the Punishments be? What would be the price being paid?

For me
- I'd not see Box of Crayons reach its full potential.

- I'd feel stuck in a role that's not my "genius work."

- I'd have great people leave the company, because I'd be a bottleneck.
- I'd lose opportunities to pursue new projects.
- I'd miss a chance to reinvent myself.

For them (Shannon, the CEO-to-be; the Box of Crayons team/culture)

- She'd miss a chance to fulfill some of her potential as a leader.
- She'd feel constrained by my leadership.
- We wouldn't be practising what we're preaching at Box of Crayons.

For us (the broader world)

- A force committed to making work better for people is diminished and reduced.

What I notice here

There's a simple, recurring theme here: the price being paid if I don't do this is a really significant loss of impact for Box of Crayons on the world.

Tipping the balance

I was never much good at science in high school.
I thought I'd have my moment of glory when I wrote an entire report on an experiment using nothing but literary quotes, my attempt to make the whole thing

less predictable and same-y than all the other reports. It was pre-Internet, so it took me *hours*, and after that labour all I got was a C-minus. Harsh.

I've become more curious about science as I've gotten older, won over by the many brilliant writers and podcasters out there. As I've read, I've (re)learned that a phase transition is the moment when matter shifts from one state to another. It's when a solid turns to liquid, a liquid to gas, and vice versa.

Two suggestions: Bill Bryson's *A Short History of Nearly Everything*. And the BBC podcast *The Curious Cases of Rutherford & Fry*.

Water's liquid at 99 degrees Celsius, and it's steam at 101 degrees. What's released in that moment of change is fascinating: enough energy to break the molecular bonds and in some ways change utterly, and in other ways change not at all (ice, water, steam... they're all still H_2O).

We face a similar moment as we examine our Worthy Goal and weigh up the Prizes & Punishments. We need the energy to break the bonds of the status quo. That happens when the Punishments (the price you and others pay for you *not* taking on your Worthy Goal) outweigh the Prizes (the comfort of things staying as they are).

So imagine this is like the weigh-in at a boxing match. Bring your best on both sides, and let's see them step on the scales.

WEIGH UP YOUR PRIZES & PUNISHMENTS, AND SEE WHICH WAY THE BALANCE TIPS

Take the best three Prizes you get if you *don't* take on the Worthy Goal. List them below in the left-hand column. Then do the same for the Punishments, and list them in the right-hand column. Which way does the balance tip?

You can do this exercise in your head, or quite possibly the whole thing feels redundant—you just know the way things have played out. All of that's fine, so long as you've got a clear enough answer.

How long will this take? Probably about five minutes.

List the best three arguments for both sides.

Comforts (Prizes)	Costs (Punishments)

Having made that list, which way does the balance tip? Towards pursuing the Worthy Goal? Or towards backing away from the Worthy Goal and sticking with the status quo?

_____

_____

_____

_____

Here's how the balance tips for me as I weigh up the
Prizes & Punishments of not taking on my Worthy
Goals. For the new podcast, the balance nudges towards
doing it... but only just. I see that if I lose sight of the
personal mission-driven reasons for doing it, it becomes
less compelling immediately and probably tips the
other way. For the second Worthy Goal, the transfer
of power, it's really clear: do it!

Which way did things tip?

It may be that the equation tips the way you hope it will.
If the Punishments of *not* taking on this Worthy Goal
clearly outweigh the Prizes of maintaining the status
quo, you're ready for the next step: Weigh Up the
Journey. Bravo, and turn the page.

But if that's not the case for you yet, don't get stuck
or discouraged. It's a success to discover this now, rather
than days, weeks, or months down the road when you
run out of motivation and mojo.

Rather, throw your hands in the air, say "How fascinating!" and get back to work. Take the off-ramp, go back to the start of the process, and rework it. There are different places you might do further exploration:

Recast your Worthy Goal. It might be a completely new aspiration, or an adjustment to the one you've been working on. This exercise might be the thing that helps you acknowledge that a Worthy Goal you've felt obliged to take on for years just might not be the right Worthy Goal for you.

Dig more deeply into the Prizes. Understand how committed you are to the way things are now.

Revisit the Punishments. See if you can feel more acutely the price you're paying by not taking on your Worthy Goal.

Time-travel ahead

If you're ready to move on, fantastic. But you're not across the threshold yet. Before you get there, you need to time-travel, see into the future, and weigh up the journey that lies ahead of you.

TIME TO WEIGH UP THE JOURNEY

SET YOUR WORTHY GOAL

↓

WEIGH UP THE STATUS QUO

↓   ↓

AMBITION WINS   **COMFORT WINS**

↓

WEIGH UP THE JOURNEY

SET A WORTHY GOAL

1 FIND YOUR FOCUS
WRITE A CRAPPY FIRST DRAFT

2 TEST YOUR AMBITION
WRITE AN ACTIVE SECOND DRAFT

3 CLAIM YOUR GOAL
WRITE A STRONG FINAL DRAFT

COMMIT

4 SEE WHERE YOU STAND
FALSE STARTS & MOSQUITOES

5 WEIGH UP THE STATUS QUO
COMFORTS & COSTS

6 WEIGH UP THE JOURNEY
QUALITIES & RISKS

CROSS THE THRESHOLD

7 TAKE SMALL STEPS
HISTORIES, EXPERIMENTS & PRACTICES

8 REMEMBER YOUR BEST SELF
THIS/NOT THAT

9 DON'T TRAVEL ALONE
BUILD THE BAND

IN THIS CHAPTER

FULLY COMMIT

TO YOUR WORTHY GOAL

6 WEIGH UP THE JOURNEY

Grow in layers

In Alexandria, Indiana, hangs the world's largest ball of paint. It started life as a baseball, and on January 1, 1977, the first coat of paint—blue—was applied. It's been painted many *many* MANY times ← since then, somewhere north of 25,000 coats. It now hangs from a beam in a purpose-built barn, has its own website, and weighs in at close to two metric tons.

For more about the ball of paint, dip into John Green's wonderful book *The Anthropocene Reviewed.*

It's not only a roadside attraction, it's a slightly awkward metaphor for how we can mistakenly think about our personal growth: another day, another barely perceivable paint layer.

Psychologist and academic Robert Kegan has one of the most robust models to describe the

111

process of self-growth. What's helpful to know for now is that, in each of his five behavioural stages, there's first growth within each stage and then a leap to the next stage.

I frame it as the difference between You+ and You 2.0. You+ is growth within the stage, and it's akin to that paint ball. You work to fine-tune yourself, getting better and more comfortable in the stage you're in. It's often everyday work: another day older, another day wiser.

You+ and You 2.0 is one way of distinguishing the difference. You can find a longer list of metaphorical pairs in a few pages.

But You+ has its limits. It's not like one of those charts where there's a straight line heading diagonally upwards. Rather, growth is an S-curve. You start slow, move more quickly up the curve, and finally begin to plateau.

To continue to grow—to unlock your greatness—you need to make the leap to the next S-curve and on to the next stage. This is You 2.0. Your Worthy Goal can be a catalyst for this leap. Your Worthy Goal can *break* the limits of You+, and free you to step into your next phase of learning and growth.

YOU+

= **FINE-TUNING**

YOU 2.0

= **LEAP TO**
THE NEXT LEVEL

A PLETHORA OF METAPHORS

Writer David Foster Wallace's commencement speech "This Is Water" begins like this:

There are these two young fish swimming along and they happen to meet an older fish swimming the other way, who nods at them and says "Morning, boys. How's the water?" And the two young fish swim on for a bit, and then eventually one of them looks over at the other and goes "What the hell is water?"

The difference between focusing on swimming and being aware of the water is one way of throwing light on the difference between You+ and You 2.0.

But I had to leave out a ton of metaphors, which killed me. I love them: they're the pictures worth a thousand words. I hoard them, like a mad squirrel. A metaphor is like a wormhole to the imagination.

Here are some of the metaphorical ways I've explained the difference between You+ and You 2.0:

YOU +	IS TO	YOU 2.0 AS
GPS	is to	orienteering with a map and compass
An app	is to	an OS (operating system)
Present You	is to	Future You
Warming water	is to	water's phase transition to steam
Le Corbusier	is to	Jane Jacobs
Newtonian physics	is to	complexity theory
Rocket ship	is to	flock of birds
Monoculture	is to	nature
Plan	is to	strategy
Direct	is to	oblique
Efficiency and progress	is to	evolution and emergence
Self-centred	is to	other-focused
Fast change (technical)	is to	slow change (behavioural)
Changing outfits	is to	morphing from caterpillar to butterfly

Wait, did you say "break"?

The whole "breaking" thing sounds fine as someone's theory, but distinctly less appealing as a process you need to go through. But scars often point to a source of strength.

To be literal about it for a moment: I have a cleft lip and palate, which means early childhood surgery left scars on my upper lip. What might be considered a weakness is something I now see as part of my "special sauce." Someone said "wisdom enters through the wound," and where we're tested and have been broken open can become a source of courage, insight, and strength.

I take comfort in the Japanese ceramic art of *kintsugi*, which translates as "golden joinery." When a dish breaks, rather than discarding it, a craftsperson beautifully repairs it with urushi lacquer infused or dusted with gold. It is a deliberate act to show rather than hide the repair. The dishes are considered more beautiful and more valuable than their unbroken companions . . . and probably more beautiful and valuable than a large, painted baseball.

But is it worth it? To weigh up the journey, you'll once again start with the Prizes. Now the question is, how might you win, what benefits might accrue, should you take on this Worthy Goal? It turns out there are external and internal benefits.

GOALS

EXTERNAL

STATUS

NEEDS

INTERNAL

QUALITIES

External: Goals and Status

The external benefits are most obvious, most shiny, and least guaranteed. You may, of course, achieve your Goal. In my case, I'd be able to say I had a top 3 percent podcast. Woohoo! Closely following that comes Status, real or imagined: I can swagger into any podcasting conference in the world; Joe, Tim, and Brené are now on speed-dial; I'm financially better off; I've got at least 10 reviews praising my insightful interviewing and ability to blend humour and compassion and insight; I've got a bunch of reviews that say both my show and I suck (truly a measure of success); my superfans have tattoos of my initials; and so on.

I'm being a little facetious, of course. You've worked really hard to craft a Worthy Goal that's Thrilling, Important, and Daunting, so you're going for important, interesting, and mostly desirable outcomes. But you may need more than these as your Prizes for undertaking this Worthy Goal.

Internal: Needs

The central mantra of this book is "you unlock your greatness by working on the hard things." To strive to become your Best Self is a lifetime's work.

To catalogue the Prizes of taking on your Worthy Goal, start by going as deep as possible, and connecting your commitment to the Worthy Goal to essential human Needs. This draws on the work of Marshall Rosenberg, creator of Nonviolent Communication, who in turn drew on the work of economist Manfred Max-Neef. Rosenberg says there are nine self-explanatory and universal human Needs:

AFFECTION	**CREATION**	**RECREATION**
FREEDOM	**IDENTITY**	**UNDERSTANDING**
PARTICIPATION	**PROTECTION**	**SUBSISTENCE**

Mostly likely, you'll be able to see the through line from your Worthy Goal to one, two, or maybe more of these essential human Needs. It will show you at a foundational level how taking on your Worthy Goal will nourish you while serving the world.

Internal: Qualities

From the foundation of Needs, we move to Qualities. If Needs are universal, your Qualities are deeply individual. There are parts of you that are already true, part of how you orient to the world when you're at your best. Taking on your Worthy Goal will amplify these Qualities. They'll be acknowledged, strengthened, brought into the light, and burnished.

This is where that phrase you've heard from me before—we unlock our greatness by working on the hard things—can chime like a clean-struck bell. This is where you start to see and acknowledge what is great about you. It's a powerful exercise, and I hope you'll give it a whole-hearted shot.

And I say that because . . . for many of us the process is a little weird, or awkward, or uncomfortable. I'm not

really one for the woo-woo, and it doesn't take much
to bring out the skeptic in me. I've got some British
friends in mind for whom this exercise is likely the acme
of their worst fears.

But it's OK. You can do this in private. You don't have
to tell anyone—it's just between you and me, and not
even me really. Just you and the book. And you've come
this far. Let's see what's there.

WHAT ARE THE QUALITIES YOU'LL BURNISH BY COMMITTING TO YOUR WORTHY GOAL?

Who would you be if you fully committed to your Worthy
Goal? This is deep work. Don't overthink it, just write down
the words that come to mind. There is a list of words to
help on the following page.

Write down up to three Needs that your Worthy Goal
would connect with and nourish.

How long will this take? Probably 10+ minutes.

Who would you be if you fully committed to your Worthy
Goal? Write down at least five words or phrases.

_____

_____

_____

_____

Which essential human Needs does your Worthy Goal
connect with and nourish?

_____

_____

_____

_____

Qualities

I am:

GENEROUS. *Brave.* **PROVOCATIVE.** *An Innovator.* **DEDICATED.**
Daring. **CREATIVE.** *Smart.* **LOVING.** *Consistent.* **DRIVEN.**
HEART-LED. *Ambitious.* **A THOUGHT LEADER.** *A Host.*
Loyal. **AN EXPERT.** *Joyful.* **CALM.** *Fearless.* **KIND.** *Restless.*
CONSISTENT. *Open.* **INSIGHTFUL.** *A Maverick.* **GENERATIVE.**
Decisive. **A FOLLOWER.** *Welcoming.* **A CONNOISSEUR.**
A STARTER. *Forgiving.* **COMPASSIONATE.** *A Champion For.*
Engaged. **RELENTLESS.** *A Learner.* **PLAYFUL.** *Trustworthy.*
INFLUENTIAL. *Catalyzing.* **AN EXPLORER.** *A Teacher.*
Dependable. **FUNNY.** *A Mentor.* **VULNERABLE.** *Confident.*
A LEADER. *With Boundaries.* **RESILIENT.** *Adventurous.*
A Bridge. **COMMITTED.**

You can "Give a Word, Take a Word" at
HowToBegin.com. If this list doesn't do
it for you, you'll find an expanded
list there.

Here's the greatness I hope these Worthy Goals will unlock in me.

Launch a new podcast that is in the top 3 percent of all podcasts within 12 months

Who would you be if you fully committed to your Worthy Goal?
The commitment would say I'm: a gatherer of people and a host; a teacher, a translator of information, a champion for making wisdom accessible; an advocate for underrepresented voices; a rule breaker and a maverick; a lifelong learner; restless; ambitious; generous; humble and confident at the same time; a creator of opportunities for others; someone who practises what he preaches.

These are really good words for me. Honestly, it thrills me to see that list. They really pass "the eulogy test": how I hope people remember me after I've died.

Which essential human Needs does your Worthy Goal connect with and nourish?
For me, the essential human Needs are: Creation and Freedom. These are almost always my two, sometimes with a dash of Identity thrown in.

EXAMPLE

Role-model a gracious, generous, and trusting transfer of power

Who would you be if you fully committed to your Worthy Goal?
The commitment would say I'm: a teacher and a mentor; a role model for how someone with privilege manages power; willing to disrupt the status quo; committed to legacy; generous; restless; ambitious.

It's interesting to see what words echo across the two Worthy Goals. Doing both of these at the same time has been helpful in reinforcing my sense of my Best Self.

Which essential human Needs does your Worthy Goal connect with and nourish?
It connects strongly to the essential human Needs of Freedom and Creation. (The same as above, but this time flipped in priority.)

Sacrifice

It's typically pretty enlivening to do that last exercise. You've seen a version of You 2.0, and I'm likely not gilding the lily to say that it's radiant and powerful.

But you can't have the light without the dark. You've articulated the Prizes, and now we have to do the same for the Punishments. They're the front and the back of the same hand. And make no mistake, you will pay a price if you take on your Worthy Goal.

One of the deep and often unspoken truths about this work is that sacrifice is required. In *The Coaching Habit* I wrote about "The Strategic Question": If you're saying yes to this, what must you say no to? "Yes" means nothing credible unless you're clear on what you'll say no to, what you'll sacrifice, to make that commitment. If you don't tally up the price that needs to be paid, you can't fully commit.

Grist for the mill

When you identified the Prizes of keeping the status quo earlier, you generated a list of what you'd maintain should you *not* take on your Worthy Goal (page 94). That's the motherlode. Go back and mine that for possibilities as you weigh up the journey. Look at material assets; your comfort (both what you have and what you don't have to face); the expectations others have of you and that you have of yourself; the way relationships currently work; your status/authority/ entitlements/privilege; your power.

As you identify what's precious to you and what might be at risk, make the potential loss explicit by claiming it. Try these sentence stubs as prompts:

- I risk...
- I perhaps would no longer...
- I might lose...
- I might be risking...
- I might be forced to give up...
- I'd have to stop hanging on to...

- I might have less/fewer...
- I'd have to acknowledge...
- I couldn't guarantee...

WHAT WOULD BE AT RISK IF YOU FULLY COMMITTED TO YOUR WORTHY GOAL?

You're seeing a theme as we work through this process: it's deep work.

How long will this take? Probably 10+ minutes.

What would be at risk if you fully committed to your Worthy Goal?

_____

_____

_____

Having made that list, what insights do you have? What patterns do you notice?

_____

_____

_____

_____

EXERCISE

Here's what's at risk for me.

Launch a new podcast that is in the top 3 percent of all podcasts within 12 months

What would be at risk if you fully committed to your Worthy Goal?

Well, let's start with time and money. I couldn't do this to the full extent without investing in a team and marketing and the like. That investment will be five or six figures, and that investment is at risk.

And there's the opportunity cost of me saying yes to this, which necessitates me saying no to other goals and dreams and opportunities. I'd lose the ability to dabble in projects and keep my options open.

And what if I don't find an audience? I might have to acknowledge that I'm not as beloved/charismatic/sure-footed as I'd like to believe.

And what if I hire some suboptimal team members? I'd run the risk of being dragged into tedious people management dynamics.

What I notice

These are familiar fears. They've been barrier enough to stop me doing things in the past, but I've eventually faced them down over time. They don't scare me any longer.

Role-model a gracious, generous, and trusting transfer of power

What would be at risk if you fully committed to your Worthy Goal?

- I risk breaking my relationship with Shannon.

- I risk breaking the company, or at least diminishing it—not just its tangible assets, but also things like reputation.

- I risk losing my Box of Crayons community: employees, contractors, and clients who enrich my life.

- I risk deciding that no one could replace me as CEO, and having myself stuck in that role forever.

- I risk anonymity and/or never being associated with something successful again.

- I risk discovering I'm not generous, that I don't like sharing or giving away power, that control matters more to me than I realize.

What I notice
The risk that feels most significant to me is the loss of my Box of Crayons community. But seeing it written down has me already thinking about what I might do to rebuild community, and that lessens the sting.

EXAMPLE

The equation

Just as you did for the Prizes & Punishments of the status quo, you once again need to look at the phase transition and see how things fall. This time, you're looking to see if the Prizes are greater than the Punishments. That will position you well for the final section, Cross the Threshold.

And if the equation doesn't work here, just like before, you celebrate. It's not failure; it's feedback. Take the off-ramp and go back and work the process until you find a Worthy Goal that generates Punishments > Prizes for the status quo and Prizes > Punishments for the journey.

WEIGH UP YOUR LISTS OF PRIZES & PUNISHMENTS, AND SEE HOW THE BALANCE TIPS

Take the best three "wins" from your work on the Prizes, the qualities in you that get released or amplified if you take on the Worthy Goal. List them in the left-hand column of the following table. Then do the same for what's at risk— the Punishments—and list them in the right-hand column. Now, which way does the balance tip?

As before, you can do this mentally or just go on gut instinct. If you know, you know.

How long will this take? Probably about five minutes.

List the best three arguments for both sides.

Qualities (Prizes)	Risks (Punishments)

EXERCISE

Having made that list, which way does the balance tip? Towards pursuing the Worthy Goal? Or towards backing away from the Worthy Goal and sticking with the status quo?

For this second weighing up of Prizes & Punishments, both of my Worthy Goals tip strongly to the doing of it. The amplification and burnishing of qualities I aspire to, in both cases, outweighs the risks.

Cross the Threshold

Even with the equations on your side, it would be a mistake to stride "confidently in the direction of your dreams," as Mr. Thoreau would have us do. You have to be smarter than that when you sally forth. You have to know how to make progress and also how to mitigate the risks you've identified. You don't want to confidently walk over a cliff edge.

And deciding how best to make progress is exactly what the next section is all about.

"Go confidently in the direction of your dreams!" Henry David Thoreau's best remembered for *Walden*, where he reflects on the qualities of a good life while living by a pond in the "wilderness" of Massachusetts, a shortish walk from the nearest town, Concord.

TIME TO CROSS THE THRESHOLD

SET YOUR WORTHY GOAL

↓

WEIGH UP THE JOURNEY

↓

UNLOCKING GREATNESS WINS

FEAR WINS

↓

CROSS THE THRESHOLD →

THRE

YOU HAVE SET A

CROSS
THE
SHOLD

WORTHY GOAL. YOU HAVE

DECIDED TO COMMIT.

NOW IT'S TIME TO

CROSS THE THRESHOLD.

Getting ready for the journey

If this were a straightforward goal, you'd be able to launch yourself into action: long, confident strides towards glory. Like Sam and Frodo setting out at the start of *The Lord of the Rings*: the sun's shining, the birds are a-twitter, they've got a tasty lunch in the backpack, ← a pipe and pipe-weed in the coat pocket. All's well and everything feels possible.

And likely a second breakfast as well.

However, your Worthy Goal isn't a stroll through the Shire. It's not even a walk in the park. You're about to journey into the unknown, and you'll need to navigate the ups and downs that lie ahead. Three principles will see you through.

1 **Take small steps.** There are three different ways to do just that, and we'll get into those in a minute.

2 **Remember your Best Self.** When doubt strikes, and it will, being able to tap into that essence of you at your best is grounding, reassuring, and empowering.

3 **Don't travel alone.** You're not Alex Honnold and this is not *Free Solo*. There's a cast of characters you'll want to gather around you to make the journey sustainable. Now, let's get cracking!

SET A WORTHY GOAL

1 FIND YOUR FOCUS
WRITE A CRAPPY FIRST DRAFT

2 TEST YOUR AMBITION
WRITE AN ACTIVE SECOND DRAFT

3 CLAIM YOUR GOAL
WRITE A STRONG FINAL DRAFT

COMMIT

4 SEE WHERE YOU STAND
FALSE STARTS & MOSQUITOES

5 WEIGH UP THE STATUS QUO
COMFORTS & COSTS

6 WEIGH UP THE JOURNEY
QUALITIES & RISKS

CROSS THE THRESHOLD

7 TAKE SMALL STEPS
HISTORIES, EXPERIMENTS & PRACTICES

8 REMEMBER YOUR BEST SELF
THIS/NOT THAT

9 DON'T TRAVEL ALONE
BUILD THE BAND

IN THIS CHAPTER

THE THREE WAYS TO MAKE PROGRESS

7
TAKE SMALL STEPS

Chocolate cake wisdom

My first job after university was in the world of product development—that's marketing-speak for inventing things. Clients would come to our agency and say something like, "We need a new frozen dessert... one as popular as Sara Lee's Double Chocolate Layer Cake!"

So we'd roll up our sleeves and get to work. We'd buy every dessert currently available and eat them ("research"), generate ideas, run focus groups (actual research), create prototypes, eat them ("research"), run more focus groups (again, actual research), and finally come back to the client with our top recommendation. Occasionally our idea would get launched. Almost always it would be a disappointing flop.

The DCLC was the undisputed monarch of frozen desserts in the UK in the 1990s, beloved by everyone aged 4 to 104.

What I now know is that the process was broken. Our ideas never really had a chance because they never really got tested. We'd just go months and months in our own little bubble, hoping to get lucky and hit the jackpot.

Meanwhile, in Silicon Valley, another innovation agency was having more success with a different approach. David Kelley, IDEO's founder, had a core axiom: fail faster to succeed sooner. That principle became gospel when Eric Ries's book *The Lean Startup* championed the idea of an MVP, a Minimum Viable Product. The essence of both is to take small steps.

Shout-out to *The Princess Bride*. Keep an eye out for flame spurts, lightning sand, and Rodents of Unusual Size.

Curiosity fuels courage

With small steps, you're doing two things. First, fuelled by curiosity, you're collecting feedback. It's the only way you can make your way forward in a complex situation: keep checking where you are, try some things out, collect feedback, and decide what's next. Second, you're mitigating risk so you don't end up plunging off a cliff or running into one or more of the three terrors of the Fire Swamp, thus prematurely ending your quest.

Jim Collins of *Good to Great* fame explains the process of figuring out strategy thus: fire bullets, then fire cannonballs. Even if you're not a fan of military

I KNOW SO MANY PEOPLE WHO FEEL HOPELESS, AND THEY ASK ME, "WHAT SHOULD I DO?" AND I SAY: "ACT."

GRETA THUNBERG

metaphors, this is helpful. Collins explains that bullets are cheap and low-risk. Firing them is a manageable commitment, one that helps you figure out the real target. Once you've identified the target, then you can fully commit and fire the cannonball. Collins says that most people don't fire enough bullets and fire their cannonball way too soon; or they spend their life firing bullets without ever having the courage to load up the cannonball.

The three ways to "fire bullets" and take small steps are: a History, an Experiment, and a Practice.

GATHER

FEEDBACK

SMALL

STEPS

REORIENT AND

RECOMMIT

Small steps: A History

The past future version of you

You've already visited the past once. When you weighed up the status quo, you noted down False Starts made on similar or related Worthy Goals. But your False Starts aren't the whole story, not by any means. You've also got stories about successes, peak moments where a best version of you rose to the occasion in just the same way you're hoping it will again.

It's like a temporal equivalent of a tongue twister.

William Gibson said, "The future is already here—it's just not evenly distributed." That's true on an individual level too. In other words—and this sounds like a trippy, back to the future, Michael J. Fox thing—You 2.0 has already shown up sometime in your past. Search your story bank, chronicle your History, and find those "peak moment" stories, moments where you were at your best. They're there. You have You 2.0 waiting to be rediscovered, recognized, and reintegrated.

That's not the only benefit. Excavating your History isn't only about catching that glimpse of You 2.0, as powerful as that is. It's also a way of better quantifying the risks you articulated in the Punishments process in "Weigh Up the Journey." It tempers our very human tendency to over- or underestimate risks by holding it up against our lived experience. You calibrate your understanding of the real risk at play. When you did that similar thing before, did that Bad Thing happen? In whole or in part?

The stories may not always be obvious, so cast around. It can be a good idea to ask someone who knows you to work with you on the History process. When I did this exercise for a friend of mine, a highly accomplished senior leader and coach, she was completely blind to examples of her past achievements, bravery, and willingness to take risks. I was able to remind her of those stories, hold up a mirror, and champion the qualities I'd seen and loved in her. What was particularly powerful, it seemed, was reflecting these qualities in the present tense—for example, "you *are* brave" (rather than "you *were* brave").

CHRONICLE A HISTORY

First, find stories from your past where a version of You 2.0 has appeared, as evidence that you're the right person for this Worthy Goal.

Second, find stories from your past that help you calibrate what's really at risk with this Worthy Goal.

I'd strongly encourage you to complete this History step. There's little to lose, and much to gain. I have a bias to action myself, and I'm not naturally drawn to reflection. But completing this exercise never fails to generate useful insights about how I've shown up in the past, and how undoubtedly I'll show up again in the future. The past is full of helpful data, data helps build confidence, and confidence helps build momentum.

How long will this take? Probably 10+ minutes.

EXERCISE

What does your History reveal about your Future Self?

_____

_____

_____

_____

_____

_____

What does your History reveal about what's at risk?

_____

_____

_____

_____

_____

_____

Here are my chronicles of Worthy Goals foretold.

Launch a new podcast that is in the top 3 percent of all podcasts within 12 months

What does your History reveal about your Future Self?

I've got a persistent story in my head that I'm a high-performing, lucky amateur. Yes, I've had some success along the way, but it's mostly because I have enough bravado to get me into the top 10 percent: a bit of skill, a bit of cheek, a good line in self-deprecating humour, and some colourful shirts. But I do most things on the cheap, with literal and metaphorical duct tape. Sometimes this self-created myth serves me well. But if I'm trying to launch a top 3 percent podcast, "lucky amateur" is not a helpful story *at all*.

However, I have another story. When I self-published *The Coaching Habit*, I committed to do it as a professional. It was an important declaration. It meant that I hired great people, produced a beautiful artifact, created time and money budgets, ran experiments and adjusted tactics as feedback came in, invested in marketing, and so on. It's the antithesis to my "bumbling amateur" story. Most of the time, though, I don't remember my "professional" story; that's why this can be such a helpful exercise.

What does your History reveal about what's at risk?

As for the risks, I can see that in every significant project I've done—my first book, my most successful book, the companies I've founded, this book you're reading right now—I've found freedom and a deep commitment to progress by confirming what I'm willing to lose. Many times what I feared I'd lose (money, time, status, opportunities), I haven't. And when I did, I understood that they're often "opportunity cost" trade-offs I chose to make.

Role-model a gracious, generous, and trusting transfer of power

What does your History reveal about your Future Self?

One of my favourite people to work with is Rob Kabwe, a designer. He's been responsible for much of the Box of Crayons aesthetic over the years, including designing some of my animated movies and most recently the How to Begin worksheet.

What I love about working with Rob is that I'll give him a brief, and he'll come back with ideas that not only deliver on the brief but go beyond what I could imagine as a solution. It's a small but powerful story to remind me that I've been able to fully trust someone with important work.

What does your History reveal about what's at risk?

Reflecting on my relationship with Rob reminds me that when things don't go quite right, there's less at stake than I worry about, and that we can always do a reset. It relies on clear, open conversation between us, but if that's there, then most things are fixable.

Small steps: An Experiment

Fire up the Bunsen burner

The Scientific Method has been one of the great boons for civilization. It's a combination of curiosity, observation, and skepticism: Here's a hypothesis. Here's a test. Here's a result. Here's a conclusion. Here's a new hypothesis. Repeat as required.

It's not an unalloyed good. We lose something when we make "provable" or "measurable" the standard for everything.

So don your white lab coat, grab a clipboard, and ideally put on a pair of safety goggles. Start to construct a one-off, contained, toe-in-the-water Experiment that will generate some useful information. You can test things like: time taken; costs involved; people's engagement (family, friends, sponsors, followers, colleagues, collaborators, audiences); your own level of engagement; the realness of Thrilling, Important, and Daunting; the repercussions of failure. You'll be creating an Experiment that makes small-step progress while mitigating risk.

As you design an Experiment, you'll need to manage three unhelpful but very human tendencies:

Making the Experiment bigger and more complicated than it needs to be. You're testing a hypothesis, an assumption you have about what will happen and what's at risk should it fail. Keep asking: What's the simplest test that would give you the data you'd find helpful?

PULL THE SWITCH!

FROM THE ANIMATED MOVIE *IGOR*

Putting too much at risk in the Experiment.
Every Experiment risks failing; the goal is to plan for a risk you can absorb. Start small. Check in: What's a micro Experiment that would provide useful data and risk little?

Investing too much in the success of the Experiment.
The purpose of an Experiment is to gather data. You win whether the Experiment succeeds or fails. "Succeed or fail" is not the measure; it's "What's the data? What did I learn from this? What does this suggest about what might be the next smart thing to do?" Whether it works or doesn't, you've already won by conducting the Experiment.

CONSTRUCT A SMALL EXPERIMENT

The goal is to gather feedback about your Worthy Goal. Ensure that you'll gain data no matter what happens, and that catastrophe won't ensue should the Experiment "fail." When you're planning your Experiment, don't worry too much about making it perfect, but do keep it small and contained. Again, you're looking to gather data, not to complete your Worthy Goal. An Experiment that didn't work is better than a perfect idea for an Experiment that's still in your head.

This can take a bit of noodling. You might want to sketch out two or three options before you choose one (feel free to draw if that suits). It can also be helpful to brainstorm this Experiment with another person.

How long will this exercise take? Probably 10 + minutes.

What hypothesis do you want to test? What's useful data to gather? How can you reduce the risk? What's the smallest Experiment?

_____

_____

_____

_____

_____

EXERCISE

Here's what's going on in the MBS lab.

Launch a new podcast that is in the top 3 percent of all podcasts within 12 months

What hypothesis do you want to test? What's useful data to gather? How can you reduce the risk? What's the smallest Experiment? Instead of just launching into everything required for a top 3 percent podcast series, one Experiment would be to create a limited series of first episodes, a collection of pilots. The pilots would help me test any number of things. Did the audience actually like my idea? What feedback did they offer on the episode? Did I actually like my idea? (I can't tell you how often an idea I've had that seemed at first glance to be the Best Thing Ever turned into Not Very Interesting At All.) How much time and money would it take? Was there an angle here that might interest a distributor or an advertiser?

An even smaller, tighter Experiment would be to write up a pitch document. I could spend time drafting a proposal for my vision for this series, then have some experts in the field review it to see if there's anything substantial here. It will take time and perhaps a bit of money, but not much else would be at risk and it would generate some very helpful data.

EXAMPLE

EXAMPLE

Role-model a gracious, generous, and trusting transfer of power

What hypothesis do you want to test? What's useful data to gather? How can you reduce the risk? What's the smallest Experiment?

I realize right away I can give Shannon some contained pieces of the CEO role. I don't have to wait and dump it all on her at a certain date. We can make it one of the more technical aspects—say, managing the profit and loss of the company—so that it's bounded, an Experiment, and there are some clear ways of measuring success and failure. We can practise recognizing success, addressing struggles, and, most importantly, keeping my fingers out of the pie.

Small steps: A Practice

How you get to Carnegie Hall

Teresa Amabile is a Harvard academic, and her book *The Progress Principle* offers up an insight that is bleedingly obvious/profound (a combination that's the mark of the very best insights): people feel good when they make regular progress on stuff that matters to them. Then, completing the positive feedback loop, when they feel good, they're more likely to make progress.

Small steps lead to good feelings lead to small steps: the virtuous circle strengthens and rises.

A Practice is a commitment to process over outcome, a commitment to taking small steps forward with the purpose of collecting feedback and learning. It's an Experiment + persistence.

A Practice differs from building a habit because it is a commitment to stay conscious and open to learning. Habit building is fundamentally about setting the goal and then putting in the reps to move a behaviour from conscious competence to unconscious competence. A Practice keeps ebbing and flowing between conscious incompetence ("I can't believe how bad I am at this! Look what I'm learning! How fascinating!") and conscious competence ("I believe I'm getting the hang of this! Look what I'm learning! How fascinating!"). ←

One person who worked through this process reflected that she'd done a lot of ad hoc Experiments to test her Worthy Goal, but hadn't really used the data to generate progress. For her, it was time to shift from an Experiment to a Practice. A Practice is really a series of controlled Experiments that build upon each other.

Annoyingly, we seem to learn deepest and fastest when we're in the discomfort of conscious incompetence.

BUILD A PRACTICE

Map out a series of steps that keeps your Worthy Goal moving forward.

The History and Experiment exercises will often open up the opportunity to declare a Practice. This is the scariest of the three exercises. The first two can be one-offs, but a Practice is by its nature a commitment. Just as with the Experiment phase, start small. Devise a small Practice you can reliably do while gathering feedback and learning.

How long will this take? Probably 10+ minutes.

What series of Experiments could you string together into a Practice? What has a degree of repetition to it but still keeps you gathering data and learning?

_____

_____

_____

_____

_____

_____

_____

EXERCISE

Here's where I'm putting in the reps.

Launch a new podcast that is in the top 3 percent of all podcasts within 12 months

What series of Experiments could you string together into a Practice? What has a degree of repetition to it but still keeps you gathering data and learning?

My podcast Practice would be about building a more nuanced understanding of just what it takes to create a top 3 percent podcast. If I considered myself "a professional podcaster," it would mean I was listening to more podcasts than I currently do, as well as taking some courses to fill in my many blind spots. My Practice is a daily immersion into the world of podcasts with a "What is this teaching me?" mindset. Another Practice is a monthly coaching session with my producer, so she can keep upping my game as an interviewer. A third Practice would be to listen to all my episodes after they've been produced. (I can't quite bring myself to do that yet, but I know it would be useful.)

EXAMPLE

Role-model a gracious, generous, and trusting transfer of power

What series of Experiments could you string together into a Practice? What has a degree of repetition to it but still keeps you gathering data and learning?

The Practice here is to set up regular meetings with Shannon to have conversations about how this transfer of power is going. I'm not sure what the best cadence might be. It could be daily, or weekly, or even monthly. But the Practice is creating opportunities for us to stop and reflect and learn.

EXAMPLE

SET A WORTHY GOAL

1 FIND YOUR FOCUS
WRITE A CRAPPY FIRST DRAFT

2 TEST YOUR AMBITION
WRITE AN ACTIVE SECOND DRAFT

3 CLAIM YOUR GOAL
WRITE A STRONG FINAL DRAFT

COMMIT

4 SEE WHERE YOU STAND
FALSE STARTS & MOSQUITOES

5 WEIGH UP THE STATUS QUO
COMFORTS & COSTS

6 WEIGH UP THE JOURNEY
QUALITIES & RISKS

CROSS THE THRESHOLD

7 TAKE SMALL STEPS
HISTORIES, EXPERIMENTS & PRACTICES

8 REMEMBER YOUR BEST SELF
THIS/NOT THAT

9 DON'T TRAVEL ALONE
BUILD THE BAND

HOW TO BEGIN

IN THIS CHAPTER

NAMING THE
VERY BEST OF YOU

8 REMEMBER YOUR BEST SELF

The best of times, the worst of times

When you're across the threshold and on the journey, your feelings can swing back and forth between light and dark. There are times when you'll be in the Csikszentmihályi flow state: every step feels assured, your confidence is unbounded, you're in the zone. Good times indeed.

Other times, doubt overwhelms you. Of *course* it does. You're on the edge of your own experience and competence. You're taking on something Thrilling and Important and Daunting. You've made a choice, which means saying yes and therefore also saying no. You've decided not to dabble, not to keep your options open, but to commit.

In those moments of doubt, you'll be feeling some cocktail of confusion, anxiety,

A state of mind conducive to productivity. Named by psychologist Mihaly Csikszentmihályi. Rumour is you pronounce his name Chicks-sent-me-high.

fear, heaviness, vulnerability, uncertainty, dread, guilt, and general dispiritedness.

That's all OK. That's normal. That's entirely expected and completely predictable. (What I'm really saying is, don't make things worse by now beating yourself up for feeling that way. Perhaps throw your hands in the air and say, "How fascinating!")

How will you go on? By reconnecting to your Best Self.

Loch don't

I mentioned earlier that my first job out of university was in product development. We didn't just work on sugary desserts. One of the agency's clients was one of the world's biggest alcohol companies. They are a behemoth, with a vast number of beers, ciders, and spirits they market to the world.

Completing the dietary holy trinity is the minor work I did on stuffed crust pizza. This is why I changed careers.

In the early 1990s, Scotch whisky hadn't yet got the status it now enjoys. It was seen as an unhip, old man's drink. Everyone from distillers to distributors sensed there was potential to grow the market, but no one had cracked it yet. My agency was tasked with solving the problem and inventing a new whisky. If the old-fashioned distilleries weren't grabbing people's attention, maybe something that spoke to the young and the cool would do the trick.

We did invent a new whisky: Loch Dhu—"the black lake" in Scots Gaelic. It was dark. It was sweet. It was horrible. It failed utterly. ScotchNoob.com describes it as "intriguingly bad, like the nasal equivalent of a horrible traffic accident." The review goes on:

Today, it has a cult and collector following, and bottles can fetch several hundred dollars apiece. Part of this fascination is due to its rarity ... and part to its reputation as one of the worst single-malt whiskies in existence.

As bad as Loch Dhu obviously was, the project was nonetheless the genesis for one of the most powerful tools I know for self-management and self-mastery. It's one I continue to use whenever I'm about to step out in front of an audience, or get down and start wrestling with work that's on the edge of my confidence and competence. I first talked about it in my book *Do More Great Work*, and I'm bringing it back out of the vaults, Disney-style, for you.

This/Not That

Think of a favourite brand of yours, a brand you feel affection and some loyalty towards. Now tell me what it is about the essence of the brand itself that makes it so different and special in comparison with its competitors.

It's a difficult thought experiment for anyone, but if you're a marketer, this is at the heart of the job. Brand essence guides what is on- or off-brand. (Peloton shouldn't launch a range of doughnuts, clearly, but should they open a dance club?) When we were trying to invent the new whisky, we ran into this challenge. What is this brand about? We found that words alone were too blunt a tool. They were too generic, too abstract, too hand-waving-you-know-what-I-mean-y.

We solved it in two ways: first, by using metaphors where possible (a picture is worth a thousand words, and a metaphor's just a grammatical name for a picture); and second, by clarifying through comparison. I've come to call this tool This/Not That. So, for Loch Dhu, instead of saying vague things about how we wanted to position it as "a cool whisky for hip young people," we would create a This/Not That table, like so:

"Originality is just unacknowledged plagiarism." Appropriately, I haven't been able to find the originator of this quote.

This	NOT	That
MYSTERIOUS	NOT	OBVIOUS
GUINNESS	NOT	MURPHY'S
DUSK	NOT	DAWN
ICE HOTEL	NOT	LOG FIREPLACE
BURBERRY	NOT	TARTAN

A richer, deeper, more specific understanding is created... It helps you to navigate and know when the vibe is right and when it's not. The tighter the comparison, the more powerful. For example, Guinness *not* Murphy's (another type of Irish stout) is more nuanced than Guinness *not* Heineken (Heineken being a lager, a different type of beer from stout).

I adapted that tool and brought it to the world of self-development and personal growth. You build pairs of words, the first one describing you at your best, the second describing when you're not quite clicking. That last distinction is important. We're not looking to contrast the highs and lows of Triumph and Disaster. We're looking for something more subtle: What manifests when you're On Your Game and when you're Slightly Off?

There are two ways to access potential content for your own This/Not That list, both helping you articulate your Best Self through lived experience. The first is to remember your past peak moments: when you felt unstoppable, in the flow state, at your edge and at your best. When you see a moment like that in your mind's eye, what do you notice about yourself? What are you doing and not doing? What's in your mind, your body, your spirit? What words or phrases or metaphors come to mind? Go from there to what "less than this" looks and sounds like, and you'll have your first draft pair.

The other way into the exercise is to flip the experience and recall moments of anxiety or tightness, moments when you felt your performance was a bit suboptimal. It's purely a subjective measure; the audience may not have noticed anything, but *you* noticed. You ask yourself the same questions. Basically, what are you noticing here? What words come to mind? Then, what's the better, more confident, more in-the-flow version of this experience? And there you have another draft pairing.

Here's an example. I was running a workshop in Connecticut. It was going well, but I was a bit on edge about it all. My co-presenter pointed out that I was leaning forward on the edge of my chair, I had my heels up off the ground and toes bent as if ready to sprint, and my right leg was (yup) jiggling. Against that, I remember the moment just before I went onstage to give my TEDx Talk. I was nervous, but I was standing still, open, breathing, rooted. For my This/Not That pair, I could write "calm anticipation *not* jiggling legs." That pairing connects back to stories and to body memory; I immediately know both states.

"How to Tame Your Advice Monster" at TEDxUniversityofNevada. Favourite comment? "Couldn't watch this because his trousers were too tight."

CREATE A THIS/NOT THAT LIST

Go for more rather than fewer pairs in the beginning (let's say, 10+). Then start fine-tuning by getting down to five to seven of your best pairs. You may want to play with different phrases and synonyms. You'll know you're getting close to being done when you get a kind of physical twitch of recognition for each of the words or phrases. That resonance often connects back to specific moments in your past, visceral experiences you can still remember.

How long will this take? Probably 10+ minutes. (As with "the eulogy test" about qualities, I've found that it doesn't take long to make a solid first draft list that's about 80 percent right, and then it takes a bunch of iterations to fine-tune it to maximum power.)

This: you at your best, at a peak moment.

Not That: you when you're 15 percent off your game—not necessarily failing, but suboptimal.

This	NOT	That
	NOT	
	NOT	
	NOT	
	NOT	
	NOT	

Having made that list, what insights do you have? What patterns do you notice?

_____

_____

_____

_____

Here are my This/Not That answers for my Worthy Goals.

Launch a new podcast that is in the top 3 percent of all podcasts within 12 months

This: at your best, a peak moment.
Not That: 15 percent off your game.

I've been working on my This/Not That list for years, so this has a ready familiarity for me. It has eight pairs of words/ phrases that I've used most often to be a better facilitator and speaker. Here are some of them:

- Step Forward *not* Step Back
- Provocative *not* Sycophantic
- Playful *not* Serious
- Smart *not* Intellectual
- "Manifesto of Insignificance" *not* "It Really Matters"

But in working on this Worthy Goal, I see that I need some new words that speak to being an entrepreneur and a founder and an investor (of money and time). A different context is asking for new This/Not That words. Here's my first draft:

- Top 3 percent *not* Amateur
- Ambitious *not* Fake-Modest

What I notice
These feel quite challenging for me, pushing me to "claim my place" in a way that's not immediately comfortable... but feels helpful nonetheless.

Role-model a gracious, generous, and trusting transfer of power

This: at your best, a peak moment.
Not That: 15 percent off your game.

Interestingly, I feel I need some new pairs of words for this Worthy Goal as well. In fact, I might need a whole new set of words here, as this is the most radical change of being and doing for me. Here are my first drafts:

- Calm *not* Reactive
- Deep Trust *not* Loose Reins
- In My Corner *not* Fingers in Pies
- Offstage *not* In the Spotlight

What I notice
It's interesting to see the theme emerge of deliberate reduction and limitation of my profile, and also of surrender.

SET A WORTHY GOAL

1 FIND YOUR FOCUS
WRITE A CRAPPY FIRST DRAFT

2 TEST YOUR AMBITION
WRITE AN ACTIVE SECOND DRAFT

3 CLAIM YOUR GOAL
WRITE A STRONG FINAL DRAFT

COMMIT

4 SEE WHERE YOU STAND
FALSE STARTS & MOSQUITOES

5 WEIGH UP THE STATUS QUO
COMFORTS & COSTS

6 WEIGH UP THE JOURNEY
QUALITIES & RISKS

CROSS THE THRESHOLD

7 TAKE SMALL STEPS
HISTORIES, EXPERIMENTS & PRACTICES

8 REMEMBER YOUR BEST SELF
THIS/NOT THAT

9 DON'T TRAVEL ALONE
BUILD THE BAND

HOW TO BEGIN

IN THIS CHAPTER

WHO SHOULD AND SHOULDN'T TRAVEL WITH YOU

9
DON'T TRAVEL ALONE

Build the Band ←

It's been said we're the sum of the five people we're closest to. Our weight, our wealth, our ambition... it's the average of their weight, wealth, ambition, and so on.

As with anything apocryphal, it's not really true. Or rather, the kernel of truth that's here has been distorted by repetition, memes, social media, and the various forces that want everything to be reductionist. Turns out, you can't blame that friend of yours for you not being as rich or as skinny as you'd like, tempting as it might be. (You're off the hook, Phil.)

Hat tip to *The Blues Brothers*. If you're Jake and/or Elwood, who's your Matt "Guitar" Murphy or Steve "The Colonel" Cropper?

But here's what *is* true. It's good to have good people around you. Particularly when you're journeying into the future.

I love that L. Frank Baum came up with the name
of the Land of Oz by glancing over to his filing cabinet
(remember filing cabinets?) and seeing the second
drawer labelled O–Z. We've all seen Dorothy strolling
down the Yellow Brick Road with her companions on
her way to the Emerald City, just as we've seen Luke
fight the Dark Side with the Rebellion, and Harry Potter
(spoiler alert) taking down Voldemort backed by the
Order of the Phoenix.

No one travels alone. Now's the time for you to
choose your travel companions.

First, who do you leave behind?

There isn't room for everyone. That's OK, because quite
frankly, you'd be better off without some of your current
companions. It's not only who travels with you on the
journey, it's also about who you choose to leave behind.

- Who in your life wants you to stay unchanging?
- Who takes more than they give?
- Who in your life sows seeds of doubt?
- Who has betrayed you and may betray you again?
- Whose idea of you is historical, rather than
  future facing?
- Who stains you with the worst thing you've done,
  rather than reminds you of the best you can be?
- Who triggers the worst in you, or at least the less
  than great?

- Who contributes to you being numb?
- Who contributes to you being afraid?
- Who colludes with you not stepping towards the Thrilling, Important, and Daunting?

These aren't small questions, and these aren't trivial decisions. There's probably an entire book—make that an Amazon subcategory—about doing this work.

WHO'S NOT NEEDED ON THIS JOURNEY?

Who do you leave behind? Start with one person. Just naming them will help. Steel your heart. Notice what comes when you name them and think of them gone... a lightness, a sense of freedom, an excited nervousness perhaps. Add others as you see fit.

How long will this take? Probably about five minutes.

Who's not needed on this journey?

_____

_____

_____

_____

_____

EXERCISE

Four directions and five friends

Indigenous traditions in North America call in wisdom from the four cardinal points. As well as having its own colour and a symbolic animal, each point has an archetypal role. These archetypes can represent qualities we want to build within ourselves. They can also represent people, wisdom, and energy that we want to have with us as we work towards our Worthy Goal.

You might think about these roles as part of your ongoing band, not just for working on your Worthy Goals. Here are my examples of people in my life who have my back.

She's also a Healer and a Teacher—but her Warrior mojo is outstanding! (I'm giving you notice: don't cross me. And you better write a good review online about this book…)

Warrior

Who has your back? Who will stand by your side? Who will step forward and hold the line? Who can help you name and channel your anger, frustration, and sadness? Who is fired with purpose? Who is fierce?

Marcella, my wife, is a great Warrior companion to me. If I've been wronged, there's no one—not even me—who's more outraged. Her fierceness gives me permission to be braver than I might otherwise be. She helps me understand boundaries and transgressions. She takes no BS and she helps me do the same.

Healer/Lover

Who brings you gentleness? Who offers you encouragement? Who provides sanctuary? Who is unconditional?
Who can help you name and channel grace and gener-
osity and acceptance?

My Brain Trust, a mastermind group I was in for
15 years, played this role for me. The five of us were
scattered across North America, and over time we devel-
oped structures to help us stay connected. We'd check
in "on the boards" a number of times per week, sometimes every day, and at a minimum once or twice a week.
We'd talk twice a month for an hour, checking in and
coaching where necessary. And we'd meet every year for
a four-day retreat.

When we started, the BT played more of a Teacher
role, helping me figure out ways to market and grow
the business I was in. That changed as each of our businesses diverged and we had less useful technical insight
for one another. Eventually, it got to a place where the
BT was somewhere I felt seen, teased, and encouraged. I
felt loved and understood.

Teacher/Magician

Who brings you insight? Who creates space for reflection? Who points out what you're missing? Who breaks
you open? Who can help you name and channel curiosity, a hunger to learn, a beginner's mind?

My friend Dr. Jason Fox is someone who plays the
Teacher role for me. He is literally a philosopher (that's
the "Dr." bit). He curates, he ruminates, he uncovers

obscurities. When I talk with him, I inevitably walk away with a new Teacher to find, new connections made, and somehow both a little smarter and a little less cocksure.

Bayo Akomolafe is another Teacher for me right now. As a maverick academic who both understands and seeks to disrupt a non-complex, Western-centric way of seeing the world, he challenges deeply and eloquently what it means to have won in this life. I know I've already won in so many ways. What does this victory blind me to? And what obligations does this victory instill in me to those who haven't been as privileged?

Visionary/Ruler

Who stretches your ambition? Who holds up great things for you? Who role-models courage and vision? Who demands better of you? Who can help you name and channel ambition, strategy, courage, a wide horizon?

The best embodiment for me right now is the team at the Business Romantic Society. Every year Tim, Till, and Monika curate an extraordinary conference, the House of Beautiful Business. They do so in a way that leaves me slightly awed. I admire their capacity for finding different voices; their willingness to experiment and take risks; and how they hold true to the principles and vision of what they do: they make business beautiful.

One more: Trickster

Beyond these four archetypes, there's another character who weaves in and out of story and fable across the universe: the Trickster. Forget the Trickster at your peril...

AT THE END OF EVERY ROAD YOU MEET YOURSELF.

S.N. BEHRMAN

Who teases you, provokes you, challenges you, mocks you? Who doesn't show you the respect you think you deserve? Who disrupts the comfortable path? Who causes chaos when you want order? Who turns things upside down? Who makes light of what's heavy and dark?

My brother Nigel occasionally plays this role for me. He's got a dry sense of humour, knows some of my vulnerabilities, and can get under my skin. He's a useful barb in times when I find myself with too much balm.

WHO DO YOU NEED AS PART OF THIS JOURNEY?

Who will you travel with? This requires some thinking and some dreaming. Specific people may come to mind. It might be "a person like X," with technical skills or a certain energy that you're looking for. You can also see from my examples above that it might not be a specific person, but an idealized person, a group of people, an organization, or another source of wisdom.

How long will this take? Probably 10+ minutes.

Who do you need with you on this journey?

Warrior

_____

_____

_____

Healer/Lover

_____

_____

_____

Teacher/Magician

_____

_____

_____

Visionary/Ruler

_____

_____

_____

Trickster

_____

_____

_____

EXERCISE

Here's my thinking about my own Famous Five.

Launch a new podcast that is in the top 3 percent of all podcasts within 12 months

Who do you need with you on this journey? When I think about this Worthy Goal, I'm in serious trouble if I'm trying to do this by myself.

Warrior: A person or a team that will fight for a quality of production which will balance out my "ah, that will do" tendency. For that, I need to find people with some technical expertise, a podcast production team that will hold me to task.

Healer/Lover: Someone who can gently keep their hand at the small of my back, a gesture that's supportive and also keeps me moving. I've got two friends in mind who are also launching or relaunching podcasts at the moment.

Teacher/Magician: Someone who will keep challenging my "high-performing amateur" shtick. Someone who can break me out of old stories and limiting beliefs, particularly about who I might best serve. Someone in my life who will hold me to a high standard, and who role-models that themselves.

Visionary/Ruler: My "Jedi Council"—guides I don't know personally, but who inspire. People like Jack White,

Stacey Abrams, Bob Dylan, Damon Albarn, and others: fearless creators and agitators. I can keep asking myself, "What would they suggest?"

Trickster: "FL," who keeps suggesting that this is a self-indulgent project.

Role-model a gracious, generous, and trusting transfer of power

Who do you need with you on this journey?

Warrior: Shannon and the team at Box of Crayons will need to hold their boundaries and stop me from stepping back into the spotlight.

Healer/Lover: Someone who can help me mourn and work through the loss of identity that comes with giving up this role. This could be a professional—a coach or therapist—but at this stage I'm thinking it might be Marcella, my wife.

Teacher/Magician: Writers and speakers about the nature of power—how it works, why we want to hold on to it, how it can subtly corrupt.

Visionary/Ruler: I need to look for CEOs who've gracefully moved out of the role and see what I can learn from them.

Trickster: "BB"—they seem to relish staying in control and they're lionized for it.

FIN

WHEN THOSE ARTY French movies come to an end, a single word appears on the screen:

— *FIN* —

As Steve Martin observed, "It's like those French have a different word for everything"... This one's for "the end."

That's an easy way to wrap things up when you're an auteur, but it's proven difficult if you're me and you've written a book called *How to Begin*. Should such a book even have an ending? Maybe I just need a single page with "To be continued..." Or have some pages that fade to black...

But it turns out I do know how to end this book. It's inspired by my dad.

Robert McTaggert Stanier

I'm writing these pages in Canberra, the city where I grew up, because Dad—everyone knows him as Robin—is in his last days. I talked about "the eulogy test" in earlier pages, and that's very much present for me as I sit by his bed.

My dad is a great man, and he's lived his life well. He's quiet and self-effacing (qualities I didn't really inherit), but make no mistake: he's lived a life of deep service. He's had Worthy Goals, and he's reached them.

To build his community. He's been on a *ridiculous* number of committees and boards, and in many volunteer roles. He's been a steady force for building coalitions, navigating around obstacles, and building legacy projects.

To celebrate and recognize people for who they are and what they've contributed. He practised people-centred leadership many years before it became a thing, and he was respected and admired in his work as an aeronautical engineer. When he retired, hundreds of people came to his farewell.

To build a family and be a role model to his sons. Dad is a kind, loyal, generous man in a strong, loving, and equal relationship with my mum, Rosey. He wholeheartedly believed in his sons. One of my first memories is of him telling made-up stories of Sir Michael, Sir Nigel, and Sir Angus riding off and having grand adventures. I'm still trying to have those adventures, and I see that inheritance in me and my brothers, Nigel and Gus, every day.

Ever greater things

On my desk, held down with a small white pebble, is a small piece of paper. On it are the final three lines of Rilke's poem "Der Schauende." Edward Snow translates the title as "The Man Watching," and the lines read thus:

Winning does not tempt him.
His growth is: to be the deeply defeated
By ever greater things.

It's an invitation that moves me deeply, and it calls me forth to be courageous and ambitious. The poem's heart is the Biblical story of Jacob, who wrestles with the angel. You never win when you wrestle with the angel; that's not the point. But it is *everything* to be doing work that matters enough that the angel meets and engages with you, the angel "who so often declined the fight."

Whoever was overcome by this Angel
(who so often declined the fight),
he strides erect and justified
and great out of that hard hand
which, as if sculpting, nestled round him.

When we take on Worthy Goals, we wrestle with the angel and it changes us. We unlock our greatness by working on the hard things.

My dad wrestled with the angel. I hope you will too.

... FOR HERE
THERE IS NO PLACE

THAT DOES NOT
SEE YOU. YOU MUST
CHANGE YOUR LIFE.

RAINER MARIA RILKE,
"ARCHAIC TORSO OF APOLLO"

ROBIN STANIER
August 3, 1938–July 17, 2021

PILOT LIGHT

WHEN I WRITE A BOOK, I keep reminding myself: write the shortest book you can that's still useful.

That results in a lot of words being cut out of the main body of the text. Some of them (most of them, in fact) are better off never seeing the light again. They're gone for everyone's betterment.

But some of the extra is useful. And that's what you'll find here.

When I thought about what to call this appendix, I had a vision of a pilot light: that small spark that serves as an ignition source for a bigger burn.

In the Pilot Light appendix you'll find:

- The How to Begin worksheet: a blank one plus example worksheets completed by real people
- Support that goes beyond the book
- Foundational books: ideas and insights on which this book is built
- References made or alluded to in the text

Thank you for taking on your Worthy Goal. You are doing something that will give more to the world than it takes, and we're better for it.

You're awesome and you're doing great.

MBS

MICHAEL BUNGAY STANIER

THE HOW TO BEGIN WORKSHEET

ON THE FOLLOWING PAGES you'll find a blank worksheet, and then two examples of it as it was completed by real people.

You'll find further examples of completed worksheets, and videos of the person working through the worksheet, at HowToBegin.com.

HOW TO BEGIN WORKSHEET

SET A WORTHY GOAL

My Worthy Goal (Thrilling, Important & Daunting)

COMMIT

False Starts   Mosquitoes (dos & don'ts)

Prizes: Comforts   Punishments: Costs

Prizes: Qualities   Punishments: Risks

CROSS THE THRESHOLD

Histories, Experiments & Practices

This/Not That

Build the Band

HOW TO BEGIN WORKSHEET
Gill Buergin: Creating a tool for girls' leadership

SET A WORTHY GOAL

My Worthy Goal (Thrilling, Important & Daunting)
I believe the world needs more female leaders. I also believe girls need our support to aspire to leadership. I want to help with that. My Worthy Goal is to write and launch a self-reflection journal for 16–18-year-old girls to explore their leadership potential. I rate this 7/7 for Important and Daunting, and 4/7 for Thrilling.

COMMIT

False Starts
I've never made a writing commitment before, so this takes me into the unknown.

Mosquitoes (dos & don'ts)
I say yes to client projects that consume attention and time, knowing I won't have time to create this journal.

Prizes: Comforts
More free time; no risk of wasting time; no sense of obligation; safety from failure.

Punishments: Costs
Girls and young women wouldn't have this resource; sense of disappointment at an unsatisfied calling.

EXAMPLE

Prizes: Qualities	Punishments: Risks
I am an ally. I am a champion for young women. I am a mentor. I am a writer.	Disappointment if it's not useful or it misses the mark; disappointment if it's just bad after a lot of time and energy is sacrificed for its creation.

CROSS THE THRESHOLD

Histories, Experiments & Practices
I have committed to a daunting goal in the past, and succeeded. It took discipline, focus, and a strong support network. It also required a supportive routine and study practice. It's helpful to remind myself I have the "stick-to-it-ness."

This/Not That
Stepping forward not resisting; being in flow not stuck; energized not burdened; striking a balance not creating pressure; connected to self not fearful of others' judgment.

Build the Band
I can name a Warrior, a Healer, and a Teacher. I need to find someone who can meet me at my boldest—a Visionary. And probably a Trickster to challenge me.

Learn more about Gill's work on her LinkedIn profile: linkedin.com/in/gillianbuerginmba.

Watch the video of Michael facilitating Gill through this process at HowToBegin.com.

HOW TO BEGIN WORKSHEET
Jorge Giraldo: Writing a first draft of his book

SET A WORTHY GOAL

My Worthy Goal (Thrilling, Important & Daunting)
To write a "crappy" first draft of a book on overwhelm
within the next 90 days and it has to have at least
20,000 words.

COMMIT

False Starts
- I've written well-received
  articles in the past, but
  I've not managed to do it
  consistently.

Mosquitoes (dos & don'ts)
- Learning about chess
  with my daughter.
- Over-researching my
  book.

Prizes: Comforts
- Spend time finding
  clients.
- Avoid the pain of writing
  a book that may not
  be read.

Punishments: Costs
- The regret of not fulfilling
  my lifelong dream.
- People will miss out
  on valuable content.

Prizes: Qualities
- I am a writer.
- I improved the quality of
  many peoples lives.
- I got a great reputation.

Punishments: Risks
- My ego may get hurt if
  the book fails.
- Valuable time may
  be lost.

CROSS THE THRESHOLD

Histories, Experiments & Practices
- Write at least 10 minutes a day, about 2,000 words per week.
- Publish two overwhelm-related articles per month to test concepts and ideas.

This/Not That
- Sailing to a destination/Not drifting in the ocean.
- A hike through the wilderness/Not a daily commute to the office.
- Daily meditation practice/Not doing the dishes.

Build the Band
- I have a Warrior, a Healer, and a couple of Teachers. I need to find a Visionary and a Trickster.
- Additionally, I have a few people, the creators, who are in a journey similar to mine, also pursuing a WG.

Learn more about Jorge's work as a coach and author at JorgeGiraldoCoaching.com.

Watch the video of Michael facilitating Jorge through this process at HowToBegin.com.

LOOKING FOR MORE EXAMPLES?

SEE FURTHER EXAMPLES of people working the How to Begin process at HowToBegin.com.

Ben Wipperman scaling a leadership program for thousands in his Fortune 100 company.

Fiona Fraser bringing for-profit and non-profit organizations together across Latin America.

Helen Townshend returning to school to do a PhD.

Kay Leigh Hagan reviving her relationship with writing.

Michelle Benning starting a foundation to support those struggling with homelessness.

Stuart Eglin managing his transition from a senior leadership position in a healthcare organization.

GO DEEPER AND MASTER THE HOW TO BEGIN PROCESS

Master the How to Begin process
How to Begin online is a self-directed course to work through and master the How to Begin process.

The program includes more than 40 short videos and real-time examples of people completing the worksheet.

Redeem the cost of the book by using the code H2B20 and get $20 off the course.

Join thousands of others who are getting the support they need for their Worthy Goals.

Learn more at HowToBegin.com

DON'T DO YOUR WORTHY GOAL ALONE

The Conspiracy
The Conspiracy is an online membership group for people who want to make progress on work that matters.

It will build courage, community, and capacity so you're best able to tackle your Worthy Goal.

It is designed around six-week "chapters" in small groups, so you have a focused period of time with a "light touch" accountability and encouragement provided by people you know.

Find out more at MBS.works

BRING WORTHY GOALS TO YOUR ORGANIZATION

How to Begin process at work
The How to Begin process can increase focus, engagement, and impact within your organization.

To bring How to Begin training to your organization, visit
MBS.works

Or email the team at
HowToBegin@mbs.works

MBS in stereo
(yes, there's an audiobook)

I've loved bringing this book to life as an audiobook. If you'd like to supplement the read with the soothing tones of my Australian-English-American-Canadian hybrid accent, you'll find the audiobook available in all the obvious places.

FOUNDATIONAL BOOKS

THE INSPIRATION for this book stretches deep and wide. But here are some of the key sources that have helped me craft this book for you.

Set a Worthy Goal

Brené Brown, *Daring Greatly: How the Courage to Be Vulnerable Transforms the Way We Live, Love, Parent, and Lead*

Brené is best known for her work on shame and vulnerability, of course. The power of her work is that when you face those things, the possibilities of a Worthy Goal become more available to you.

Jacqueline Novogratz, *Manifesto for a Moral Revolution: Practices to Build a Better World*

Jacqueline founded Acumen, which combines the disciplines of a venture capitalist with a commitment to provide funding for initiatives that are changing the world for the better. This book is full of great stories, but what sticks with me most is her call to action: give more to the world than you take.

Rainer Maria Rilke, "The Man Watching," translated by Edward Snow

This is the poem I've come back to and back to and back to as I've written this book and as I've set about creating Worthy Goals for my work at MBS.works.

Commit

Robert Kegan and Lisa Laskow Lahey, *Immunity to Change: How to Overcome It and Unlock the Potential in Yourself and Your Organization*

Bob and Lisa's book builds on the work of Ron Heifetz. It was part of the foundation of my work around Easy Change and Hard Change (which I talk about in *The Advice Trap*), which this book was originally about. *How to Begin* changed focus as I wrote it, but this book nonetheless deserves its place here.

The Austin Kleon trilogy: *Steal Like an Artist · Show Your Work! · Keep Going*

Austin continues to be someone I look up to, not only for what he writes and creates, but for how he shares it with the world.

Cross the Threshold

Seth Godin, *The Dip: A Little Book That Teaches You When to Quit (and When to Stick)*

I could have named about five of Seth's books here. He's a great champion for making a ruckus in the world. I've picked *The Dip* because it's about keeping going when it's hard to keep going.

Ryan Singer, *Shape Up: Stop Running in Circles and Ship Work That Matters*

In this book, Ryan, the former Head of Strategy for the product company Basecamp, explains in helpful detail the process that company has built to make meaningful progress on projects.

REFERENCES AND ALLUSIONS

p. ii   Strictly Ballroom *is the only movie*... Baz Luhrmann directed *Strictly Ballroom* (1992), the first of what he calls the Red Curtain Trilogy. The other two are *William Shakespeare's Romeo + Juliet* (1996) and *Moulin Rouge!* (2001).

p. iii *Kevin Kelly created the Death Date*... "My Life Countdown," kk.org/ct2/my-life-countdown-1/.

p. 14   *David Brooks talks about this*... *The Second Mountain: The Quest for a Moral Life* (2019).

p. 15   *Perhaps you're what Minda Harts calls*... *The Memo: What Women of Color Need to Know to Secure a Seat at the Table* (2019). Minda's also been a guest on the *2 Pages with MBS* podcast.

p. 20   *In Jacqueline Novogratz's wonderful book*... This is the brilliant call to action in *Manifesto for a Moral Revolution: Practices to Build a Better World* (2020). Jacqueline has a wonderful TED Talk based on the same themes.

p. 22   *They're two hands stretching a rubber band*... Robert Fritz, *The Path of Least Resistance: Learning to Become the Creative Force in Your Own Life* (1984).

p. 27   *David Allen's book*... *Getting Things Done: The Art of Stress-Free Productivity* (2001).

p. 30   *I first heard "shitty first draft"*... Anne Lamott, *Bird by Bird: Some Instructions on Writing and Life* (1994). Also see Brené Brown, *Rising Strong: How the Ability to Reset Transforms the Way We Live, Love, Parent, and Lead* (2015).

p. 33   *Without wanting to go all* L'Étranger *on you*... Albert Camus, *L'Étranger* (*The Stranger*) (1942). Existentialism with a dash of absurdity.

p. 58   *1,000 true fans*... "a thousand true fans" is a phrase coined by Kevin Kelly.

p. 60   *I read a provocative article*... Dan Luu, "95%-ile Isn't That Good," danluu.com/p95-skill/.

p. 73 *Dave Snowden's a Philosopher King...* If you're interested in complexity, adaptability, the Cynefin model, and more, you might consider exploring Snowden's Cognitive Edge Network.

p. 73 *Back in October 2020 Dave tweeted...* @snowded, twitter.com/snowded/status/1316589975207645186.

p. 85 *Inner Critic or Gremlin...* Rick Carson, *Taming Your Gremlin: A Surprisingly Simple Method for Getting Out of Your Own Way* (1983).

p. 85 *When Outkast sang, "Now throw ya hands in the air..."* "ATLiens," *ATLiens* (1996).

p. 85 *Ros and Ben Zander, co-authors of* The Art of Possibility... *The Art of Possibility: Transforming Professional and Personal Life* (2000).

p. 86 *Elizabeth Lesser's book... Cassandra Speaks: When Women Are the Storytellers, the Human Story Changes* (2020).

p. 97 *Language from the Karpman Drama Triangle...* Stephen R. Karpman, *A Game Free Life: The New Transactional Analysis of Intimacy, Openness, and Happiness* (2014).

p. 103 *Bill Bryson's* A Short History... *A Short History of Nearly Everything* (2003).

p. 111 *John Green's wonderful book... The Anthropocene Reviewed: Essays on a Human-Centered Planet* (2021). The podcast of the same name is even better than the book.

p. 111 *Psychologist and academic Robert Kegan...* Kegan's books are *The Evolving Self: Problem and Process in Human Development* (1983) and *In Over Our Heads: The Mental Demands of Modern Life* (1998). In *The Listening Society* (2017), Hanzi Freinacht's framing of Kegan's model is helpful.

p. 112 *Rather, growth is an S-curve...* Whitney Johnson writes compellingly about how the S-curve, originally a mathematical term and then an economic one, applies to self-growth. Her latest book is *Smart Growth: How to Grow Your People to Grow Your Company* (2022).

p. 114 *David Foster Wallace's commencement speech...* Wallace's 2005 speech at Kenyon College can be read or listened to at fs.blog/2012/04/david-foster-wallace-this-is-water/.

p. 118 *This draws on the work of Marshall Rosenberg... Nonviolent Communication: A Language of Life* (2003).

p. 130 *"Go confidently in the direction of your dreams!"...* Henry David Thoreau, *Walden* (1854).

p. 135   *Like Sam and Frodo...* J.R.R. Tolkien, *The Lord of the Rings* (1955).

p. 135   *You're not Alex Honnold... Free Solo* is the extraordinary 2018 film of the first free solo climb of famed El Capitan's 900-metre vertical rock face at Yosemite National Park.

p. 140   *Eric Ries's book... The Lean Startup: How Today's Entrepreneurs Use Continuous Innovation to Create Radically Successful Businesses* (2011).

p. 140   *Jim Collins of* Good to Great *fame... Good to Great: Why Some Companies Make the Leap... and Others Don't* (2001).

p. 143   *William Gibson said... The Economist*, December 4, 2003.

p. 146   *Here are my chronicles of Worthy Goals foretold...* Gabriel García Márquez, *Chronicle of a Death Foretold* (1981).

p. 147   *Rob Kabwe, a designer...* PopLogik.com. Check out his online games *Nimian Legends* and *Wilderless*.

p. 152   *Teresa Amabile is a Harvard academic...* Teresa Amabile and Steven Kramer, *The Progress Principle: Using Small Wins to Ignite Joy, Engagement, and Creativity at Work* (2011).

p. 159   *The best of times, the worst of times...* Charles Dickens, *A Tale of Two Cities* (1859).

p. 159   *There are times when you'll be in the Csikszentmihályi flow state... Flow: The Psychology of Optimal Experience* (1990).

p. 161   *ScotchNoob.com describes it as...* "Loch Dhu (10 Year)," scotchnoob.com/2011/01/26/loch-dhu-10-year/.

p. 161   *I first talked about it in my book... Do More Great Work: Stop the Busywork, and Start the Work That Matters* (2010).

p. 171   *If you're Jake and/or Elwood... The Blues Brothers* (1980).

p. 172   *I love that L. Frank Baum came up with the name of the Land of Oz... The Wonderful Wizard of Oz* (1932).

p. 175   *My friend Dr. Jason Fox...* DrJasonFox.com.

p. 176   *Bayo Akomolafe is another Teacher for me...* BayoAkomolafe.net.

p. 176   *Business Romantic Society...* HouseOfBeautifulBusiness.com.

p. 180   *Famous Five...* Enid Blyton's 21 books in the Famous Five series (Julian, Dick, Anne, George, Timmy the dog).

p. 185   *Edward Snow translates the title as "The Man Watching"...* Read the English translation of Rainer Maria Rilke's poem here: poems.com/poem/the-man-watching/.

GRATITUDE

WHEN WINNERS GIVE their speech at the Oscars, they've only got 60 seconds, so of course they're not going to be able to mention everyone involved. As an author, you've got as much paper as you want, which makes the inevitability that I'll forget some important person all the worse. But let me plunge in. And if it's you I've forgotten, my apologies.

The Box of Crayons team, and in particular Dr. Shannon Minifie, who's an even better CEO than I dreamt possible.

The MBS.works team, in particular Ainsley Brittain, Head of The Conspiracy.

The *2 Pages with MBS* podcast team: our major-domo Tugba Yeniay, and One Stone Creative: Megan Dougherty and Audra Casino.

The Page Two team. It's been five years since I first worked with this generous, ambitious group of people, and they only get better. I regularly get asked to get on calls with people so they can find out what it's *really* like to work with them; and I reply: no point, because there's nothing to say other than I trust them completely. Amanda balances great patience, insight, and persistence as my editor. Lorraine is a force for change in sales. Gabi does a brilliant job running the show. Meghan is starting to reinvent book marketing. Peter designs with flair. (The book's cover, Peter's idea, is my favourite yet: elegant, witty, and an homage to Italo Calvino's *If on a Winter's Night a Traveller*. And did you pick up the nod to Maurice Sendak's *Where the Wild Things Are*?) Jesse, the co-founder, has a heart as big as a whale.

I'm grateful for those who've pointed the way to writing wisdom with heart. Nick Cave, whose The Red Hand Files newsletter is a marvel. Paul Kelly, who can tell a story without a wasted word. John Green, whose *The Anthropocene Reviewed* podcast is luminous. Brené Brown, for the gift of being on her podcast.

My early reader group: Ainsley Brittain, Dr. Chantal Thorn, Dad, Eric Klein, Erin Naomi Burrows, Gabrielle Lewis, Gus Stanier, Jason Fox, Jenny Blake, Karen Wright, Kate Lye, Loraine Santos, Mary Sheldon, Misha Glouberman, Octavia Goredema, Padraig "Pod" O'Sullivan, Phil Dooley, Dr. Shannon Minifie, Stefanie Harrison, Tim Leberecht, Tom Wujec, and, of course, Marcella, *primus inter pares*.

The hundreds of people, part of the community at MBS.works, who participated in sessions I ran in early 2021. When you watch a comedy special on Netflix or HBO, what you're seeing is material that's been honed and tweaked and refined in clubs around the country, before finally being filmed and set in amber. This lovely group of people helped ensure that the ideas and processes in this book have engaged with reality. Thank you particularly to the generous individuals who've shared their How to Begin worksheets (and lives) with us all: Ben Wipperman, Fiona Fraser, Gill Buergin, Helen Townshend, Jorge Giraldo, Kay Leigh Hagan, Michelle Benning, and Stuart Eglin.

This book is inspired by Dad. This book is dedicated to Marcella.

ABOUT MICHAEL

MICHAEL BUNGAY STANIER distills big, complex ideas into practical, accessible knowledge for everyday people so they can be a force for change. Ironically, his surname—Bungay Stanier—is anything *but* simple, which is why he often goes by the moniker MBS.

Michael's books have sold over a million copies, and *The Coaching Habit* was a *Wall Street Journal* bestseller. He has been featured on the blogs and social media platforms of thought leaders including Seth Godin, Tim Ferriss, and Brené Brown; has appeared on ABC, BBC, CBC, and innumerable podcasts; and has been featured in various publications including *Harvard Business Review*, *Forbes*, and *Fast Company*. His TEDx Talk on Taming Your Advice Monster has been watched more than a million times.

MBS is the founder of Box of Crayons, a learning and development company that helps organizations transform from advice-driven to curiosity-led action. They have trained more than half a million people for clients including Microsoft, Salesforce, TELUS, and Gucci. You can start a conversation with them at BoxOfCrayons.com.

Before he established Box of Crayons, MBS's accomplishments included publishing an academic article on James Joyce and at about the same time a Harlequinesque short story; playing small roles in helping invent Pizza Hut's stuffed crust pizza and creating "one of the worst single-malt whiskies in existence"; and spending 20 minutes dashing off what has remained GlaxoSmithKline's global vision for more than 20 years.

A Rhodes Scholar, MBS is an Australian who lives in Toronto, Canada.

You can join others who want to be a force for change at MBS.works.

You're awesome and you're doing great.